Who Decides What the Bible Means?

WHO DECIDES WHAT THE BIBLE MEANS?

Ken Schenck

CafeTutor Publishing
Marion, Indiana

CafeTutor Publishing
Marion, Indiana

All translations of Scripture are the author's unless otherwise noted.

ISBN 978-0-6151-5744-3

www.kenschenck.com

To my persevering wife, Angie

Who Decides What the Bible Means

Contents

Introduction

Sally was baptized in a Roman Catholic Church as a child. But a few months later her parents started attending a Greek Orthodox Church. While the new priest accepted her Catholic baptism, he told her parents she had not been baptized correctly. He argued that a child should be immersed under water three times in the name of the Father, Son, and Holy Spirit. The Catholics had poured water over her head once in the name of Jesus Christ. Consequently, her parents had her baptized again.

When Sally became a teenager, she attended a Baptist Church. There she was told that her childhood baptism didn't count because she wasn't old enough to know what she was doing. They urged her to say a prayer they called the "sinner's prayer," to "ask Jesus into her heart" so she could be "saved," and to be baptized again—certainly by immersion.

In college she went to a Lutheran Church. When the minister found out she had been baptized not only twice, but three times, he was horrified. Come to find out, a few centuries ago some Lutherans and Catholics even put people to death who practiced rebaptism of this sort.

Finally, in her adult life she found herself attending a Friends Church in the Quaker tradition. She was almost afraid to ask what they thought about baptism. When she finally brought up the subject, the pastor replied softly, "Oh don't worry. Baptism isn't an essential part of a Christian's life. Most of us in this church have never been baptized."

Baptism is only one of countless issues over which Christians of various groups disagree. While this story is fictitious, it illustrates a common experience. We often find that different Christian groups have strong beliefs that contradict the strong beliefs of other Christian groups.

Such disagreements are often so sharp that one group will "de-Christianize" the other. That is, they will not even consider people from other groups to be Christians. The result is over 20,000 denominations or organized Christian groups in the world. Needless to say, non-Christians often find it hard to believe that Christianity is the path to truth when Christians themselves disagree to such a great extent.

What is even more intriguing is the fact that the vast majority of these groups are Protestant churches that strongly claim to get their beliefs and practices from the Bible. Many Christians not only believe that the Bible is the ultimate authority for a Christian. In many cases they teach that the Bible is the *only* true authority for a Christian. Like Martin Luther, the father of Protestantism, such groups claim that "Scripture alone" is a sufficient basis for Christian belief.

This situation raises a number of crucial questions for us as Christians. For example, even if we belief that the Bible is absolutely authoritative over us— which Bible? That is, which interpretations of the Bible are the truly authoritative ones? Is there one Christian group that has it right, while all the others have it wrong? Or do most Christian groups have *some* things right as well as some things wrong?

I myself come from a relatively small Christian group in the Methodist tradition.[1] I remember having a conversation with someone once in which I was talking about some of the things we believe in our tradition. The person immediately objected to the word *tradition*. She didn't think I should think of our beliefs as a tradition. Rather, "we just read the Bible and do what it says."

Indeed, I used to think this same way. I used to be amazed that I just happened to be born into the group that had the *correct* understanding of the Bible and God—out of all the different Christian and non-Christian faiths out there. I still have confidence in the basic beliefs of my tradition, but I also recognize the vast number of cultural and historical influences that have helped shape why we think the way we do.

Clearly there must be more to it than the simple "I just read the Bible and know what it says" approach. After all, when thousands of individuals are taking this approach and coming up with widely different interpretations, something else is obviously going on in the process. This observation leads us back to the central question of this book: who decides what the Bible really means? With so many contrasting interpretations, how can we know which ones are correct?

Someone might suggest that God will show us if we are truly listening. But this answer doesn't work. We find truly godly people in every church and denomination. The more people you know from other traditions, the more you realize that no church has a corner on spirituality. For whatever reason, God just doesn't correct all our misunderstandings. If God did, there would be one group to which all the truly holy people belonged. No such group exists.

So maybe we should go with Catholic and Orthodox interpretations, since these groups have been around the longest. After all, these were practically the only Christian groups for almost 1500 years! Until the split between east and west in 1054, the only real option for the overwhelming majority of Christians was Catholic. And from the split until the Protestant Reformation of the 1500's, the Roman Catholic and Orthodox traditions were basically it. Do we really suppose that God had no part in any of the beliefs Christians had for the majority of Christianity's history?

Yet it is equally clear that the beliefs and practices of the Roman Catholic Church in 1500 included some significant differences from those of Christians at the beginning. Protestants have long pointed out this fact and tried to "get back" to what the first Christians believed, particularly as found in the Bible. Some Protestants see the continuity of "true" belief in smaller groups throughout history who were persecuted by the church at large.

But of course these groups also differed widely from each other in belief and practice. And if the solution is to "get back" to what the first Christians believed, then we are right back to our problem. Whose interpretation of the New Testament is the one that truly represents what the first Christians believed?

> More foundational than the question of *whether* the Bible is authoritative is the question of *which interpretation* is authoritative.

So who decides what the Bible means? Far more foundational than the question of *whether* the Bible is authoritative over us is the question of *which interpretation* is authoritative. Standing in the background of our problem are some very basic aspects of language. These aspects of language are fairly simple to grasp, but they have incredible consequences for those of us who read the Bible.

The Root of the Problem

At the heart of our puzzle is the incredible flexibility of words and the fact that we are often unaware of it—especially when it comes to the Bible. After all, words are only squiggles on a page or sounds in the air. They are "signs" that point to meanings. These meanings ultimately aren't really in the words themselves but in the mind of the person reading or hearing them.

Let's look at the problem at its bleakest. Ultimately, the meaning we find in a word depends completely and utterly on the "dictionary" we bring to the word.[2] It is not in the word itself. And the way I define words will often differ from the way someone else defines them. In a sense there are potentially as many different interpretations of the Bible as there are people reading it.

This situation in part relates to what is called the "egocentric predicament," the fact that we are all stuck inside our own heads. I am often amazed at how differently I look at the world from others around me, even those closest to me. The stereotypical differences between male and female understandings of the world are notorious, the stuff of legends and sitcoms. People often try to understand each other—I'm willing to say they regularly succeed. But to some extent, I'll never be able to get fully into your head to think exactly the way you do.

The meaning of the Bible is not inserted directly into my head, like something that comes already installed on the hard drive of my computer. Its meaning has to be "input-ed" from the outside. As soon as I reflect or try to understand this meaning, I am using thought. Even if God reveals a truth to me, my understanding of that revelation involves my thought and experiences. In other words, my faltering human reason is *always* involved when I am interpreting Scripture.

It is only when two people are operating from a common "dictionary" that they will have the

> My faltering human reason is *always* involved when I am interpreting Scripture.

same interpretation. When two Baptists are reading the Bible, there's a much better chance they will see the same meaning than when a Baptist and a Catholic are comparing notes. We can communicate to each other today because there is such an incredible overlap in the way we define words. If I talk to you about a "show" I saw on television, you will probably understand me. You probably have a television and have watched a program on it at some point. We have common "entries" into our dictionaries, allowing us to understand one another.

But people from a hundred years ago would not initially understand our conversation. They would not have seen a television or know what such a show was. We would have to make a new entry into their dictionary for them to understand us. To accomplish this goal, we would find meanings we had in common and then build from there.

In some ways I am painting a bleaker picture than is actually the case. While meaning ultimately takes place in my mind, there is often something "real" outside my mind to ground my understanding. So while words are signs, they often point to things in the real world—cats, dogs, etc. In other words, the world gives us a number of basic meanings in common with others from the outset of our quest for understanding.[3]

But even this "help" to understanding doesn't ensure that we will understand each other. We may all know what a dog is in general, but different cultures think and talk about dogs in different ways. Are we talking to a upper middle class American dog-lover who puts their poochy in a dog hotel when she goes on vacation—or even insists on taking it with her? Are we talking to a third world person who would sooner let chickens come into the house than that skin-and-bones dog that wanders around scrounging for food?

And what do you picture in your mind when you see the word *the* or the word *righteousness*? In other words, there often *isn't* anything concrete in the world that corresponds to a word. What does a "wild goose chase" really have to do with a goose or a chase in the end? Most people use this phrase without any thought of a goose.

So we define words on the basis of how they are used, not because of some universal, timeless dictionary or because they correspond to

> The meaning of a word depends on how it is used in a specific context. Words do not correspond neatly to things in the world or to some universal, timeless dictionary.

something concrete in the real world. The meanings of words thus vary depending on the situations in which they are used. We give meanings to words depending on their *context*. When two people read a word against the same context, they will see the same meaning.

For example, you need a context to know whether the word *rock* means a stone or whether it is talking about moving something back and forth, to *rock*. Is a tire *flat* or are you talking about your apartment, your *flat*? Is your steak *rare* or is it a *rare* book? Is adultery *bad* or is someone "bad" in the way of Michael Jackson's well-known song?

The different meanings of a word may have nothing to do with one another. They often do not have some central, essential meaning that plays itself out every time the word is used. We "define" a word by how we think it is being used in a specific situation.

A dictionary thus does not *tell* us what a word means, as if the dictionary is truly the authority behind meaning. A dictionary provides us with a list of the ways in which a word is being *used* at any given point in history, listed from most to least frequent. In other words, *we collectively* tell the dictionary what words mean by the way we are using them. For this reason dictionaries have to be updated regularly as words take on new meanings and other meanings fall out of use.[4] And there ain't nothing our English teachers can do to stop this process of change.

So words do not have fixed meanings inside them. Words are signs by which minds understand meanings. The meanings we find in words depend completely on the "dictionary" we bring to the words. This fact alone creates a situation in which there are potentially as many different understandings of the Bible's words as there are persons reading it.

We construct our "dictionaries" on the basis of how we use words, which in turn is a function of how the people around us are using words. Again, words do not have fixed meanings that play themselves out every time a word is used. The "definition" we apply to a word depends on the context in which we think it is being used.

We can now reformulate the fundamental question of this book: "Who decides what the Bible means?" A more accurate question would be "What is the right dictionary to bring to these words so that they take on authoritative meanings?" Or even more accurately still, "What is the right context in which to read the Bible's words so that they take on authority, the authoritative way to "use" the words?"

We bring all these meanings with us to the text from outside the text. As we will see, the idea that we base our beliefs on "Scripture alone" often reflects a misunderstanding of how words work, especially when we take into account the way the words of the Bible came together.[5] Technically, no one has ever interpreted Scripture on the basis of the text alone. The meaning we find in the words depends completely and utterly on things *we* bring to the text.

> The idea that we might base our beliefs on "Scripture alone" often reflects a misunderstanding of how works work and of how its books came together.

When we understand this truth, the incredible diversity among Christians claiming to base their beliefs solely on the Bible makes perfect sense. The diversity of interpretations is a natural result of the ambiguity of language in general. Now combine this situation with the fact that so many are unaware of the factors leading them to their interpretations—and the fact that they think they speak directly for God! This is a recipe for the so-called "Protestant principle": Protestant groups will split and split again as each group finds the "real" truth in their reading of Scripture alone. Once we understand this situation, we will never be able to read the Bible the same again.

Potential Dictionaries

So which dictionary unlocks the authoritative meaning of the Bible? "God's dictionary" is of course the correct answer, but not an immediately helpful one. Who can tell me what God's dictionary says? My minister or priest? Then what happens when the minister down the street gives me different definitions than my minister? In other words, we are right back where we started. If "God's dictionary" was this obvious, all godly people would agree on what the Bible means. They don't.

So what are some possible dictionaries a person might use to define words—any words? We each certainly start off life with a dictionary that is a unique combination of entries from our broader culture and our specific lives. If I am an American or someone from a particular American sub-culture, my context will provide me with a host of ways of thinking and talking about the world. My family and immediate circumstances will supplement these.

Will I find the right "dictionary" among these entries? Certainly God can meet me in these definitions, "stooping to my weakness," as it were. A good

English translation of the Bible will try its best to find English words and phrases that at least have similar meanings to those the Bible had originally. Ideally, this effort at least gets us in the ballpark.

Those of us who grew up in a particular church often bring with us yet another "dictionary" to the Bible—the dictionary of our Christian tradition. If you are a Baptist or a Catholic or a Methodist, certain verses will stand out to you as you read. There will be words that take on significance because they have special meaning in your tradition.

Will I find the right dictionary among these entries? Perhaps you will. Certainly God can meet you in these definitions. But remember our opening illustration of Sally? Remember how much these traditions differ from one another? In other words, traditional dictionaries do not give us a fixed, rock-solid meaning of the Bible on which to stand.

Another dictionary we might bring to the text is the "original meaning" dictionary. Here we refer to the meaning these words had when they were first written. While we will often have difficulty knowing this meaning, it is in theory more stable than any of the others we have mentioned up to this point.

The Bible wasn't originally written in English, and it was not a single book written at one time. God did not get all the Bible's authors together one day and start dictating to them. If we take these books seriously, *they* say they were written to various ancient audiences like Romans, Corinthians, Thessalonians, and Israelites. In other words, these books did not originally address anyone alive today directly. We should allow for the possibility that some biblical prophecies were intended for our time, but such instances would clearly be the exception rather than the rule.

So if God inspired Paul to write to the ancient Corinthians, surely he

> The books of the Bible did not *originally* address anyone alive today.

wanted them to understand the message. If so, then the dictionary we need in order to understand the original meaning is the dictionary of Paul and an ancient Corinthian Christian. What would the Greek words behind our English translations have meant to someone living in ancient Corinth who was part of the Christian gathering there in the mid-50's AD?

We do not come equipped with the cultural dictionary of ancient Corinth or with the special dictionary of the ancient Corinthian church. We would have to make extensive entries into our "dictionary" to come anywhere close to understanding the precise nuances a book like 1 Corinthians had originally. Indeed, the full dictionary of the Corinthian church is lost to time. While we are on earth we will never be able to know with absolute certainty the exact nuances of the Corinthian letters!

> We would have to make extensive entries into our "dictionary" to come anywhere close to understanding the precise nuances a book like 1 Corinthians had originally.

The same is true of every book of the Bible. We would have to make extensive entries into our dictionaries about ancient history, literature, and culture before we could even come close to knowing the original meaning and connotations of each book. And even when we have exhausted every speck of information available to us, we will still lack sufficient information to reconstruct the original meaning with absolute certainty.

Even when we feel relatively confident about the original meaning, we still have to connect the particular teachings of each book to those of the others. These books originally addressed widely differing cultures and situations over a thousand year period. In other words, they each used at least a slightly different dictionary than the others. The books themselves largely do not tell us how to connect these teachings to one another.[6] This task is once again something *we* do from the outside of the text looking in. We all construct an overall meaning on various issues that somehow filters and integrates the particular teachings of each book.

We must then bridge the gap between these ancient contexts and our current one. If the meaning of a word or command has everything to do with its context, then we face the task of "translating" the Bible's commands to address our context. Doing what they did would not be doing what they did unless it has the same meaning in our context as it did in theirs. We will often find that this is not the case.

Once again, the Bible may give us hints, but it does not tell us directly how to re-apply its principles to today. Philippians tells us it was addressed to

> Doing what they did would not be doing what they did unless it has the same meaning in our context as it did in theirs.

Christians at Philippi. It never says anything like "and for those who will live in America in the 21st century, here's how these principles would play out"! The process of appropriating Scripture is something we do looking at the text from the outside. We will set out the complexity of our situation in the rest of this book.

What we are increasingly seeing is that the Bible ultimately is not the controlling factor in what a Christian believes. We have found nothing but instability to the meanings the Bible might have. And the most stable one of all—the original meaning—is the one that seems least directly relevant to our world. Until the church acknowledges the other factors guiding our interpretations—our traditions, our cultures, our individual lives—we will be in great danger of mistaking the voices in our heads for God's voice.

> The Bible ultimately is not the controlling factor in what a Christian believes.

I do have one other dictionary to suggest for this equation. We might call it the "dictionary of the church" or the "dictionary of Spirit speaking through the church." It is not a perfectly stable meaning, but it seems to have several fixed points, and by its very nature it is directly relevant. By the dictionary of the church I refer not to the beliefs of individual traditions but to the beliefs and practices that are the general consensus of the vast majority of Christians, what is sometimes called the *consensus fidei*, the "consensus of faith."

Although many of us are often painfully unaware of them, Christians agreed on a number of creeds in the first few centuries of the church. I would argue that the original audiences of the New Testament would not have easily understood our belief in the Trinity. But the Trinity is an entry in the dictionary of the church. It is thus appropriate for Christians to read the Bible with the Trinity in view, even though it was not a part of the original meaning.

Christians hold generally to a number of other beliefs and practices as well. Most Christians believe that God created the world out of nothing, even though this is not the clear teaching of the Bible's original meaning or of the earliest Christians. But the dictionary of the church makes it legitimate to read the Bible's words in this way. The Bible nowhere argues for the abolition of slavery, yet most Christians today see slavery as contrary to the Christian faith. The anti-slavery position has come to be part of the dictionary of the church within the last two hundred years!

We will have recourse later to discuss how a Christian might legitimately draw on all the various dictionaries we have suggested. The next chapter discusses what we might call "individual" or "personal" dictionaries, very private meanings people find in the words of the Bible. Following it is a chapter on the dictionaries of various church traditions, "traditional" or "denominational" dictionaries. It presents some of the unique ways that different church groups interpret the Bible. Chapter three then shows how culture can affect the meanings we find in a text.

Following these chapters we finally ask whether an "original meaning" dictionary might hold the key for how to read Scripture. In particular, we ask about the dictionaries scholars bring to the words of the Bible. After a taste of the field, we are left wondering whether the original meaning is really the "be all and end all" of Scriptural meaning. Biblical scholarship often leaves us asking if there isn't more to the Bible than the dissection of texts with ancient meanings.

I finally suggest what a "dictionary of the church" might look like, particularly one that is focused on the way in which God's Spirit has and continues to work in the people of God as a whole. Such a dictionary would have to allow both for development in the way God has revealed truth throughout the centuries, as well as for the possibility that some eras of

Christian thought are passing phases of revelation. It would have to allow for misguided periods of understanding as well and for the possibility of correction and reversal. The church will have to tell me whether its Spirit resonates with these thoughts.

---

[1] The Wesleyan Church.

[2] I am using the word *dictionary* in a very loose sense here. As we will see, the meaning of a word is really a function of the context in which it is used and is technically not a matter of one-to-one definition.

[3] All human brains also share a great deal of "physiological" common ground, which includes basic categories by which we process the world (e.g., space, time, cause-effect).

[4] Even the wording of the King James Version was revised up until the late 1700's. This fact is one of the many reasons why it is inappropriate to insist that Christians only use one version of the Bible.

[5] This was one of Martin Luther's fundamental principles as he protested aspects of the Roman Catholic Church. Of course he did not "use" the term *sola scriptura* in exactly the way we are.

[6] Sometimes they do. Several New Testament writings tell us how to connect their teaching to that of the Old Testament.

Chapter 1
When Individuals Decide

Impressions from God

The missionaries had just returned from a year in Haiti.[1] They were visiting churches that had supported them financially and with prayer. When they came to my church, I was fascinated with the way they used some verses from the Old Testament to talk about their work.

Even before they were married, the couple felt that God had "given" them some verses from Ezekiel. They believed that this passage held hidden meaning for what God was going to do with their ministry. The verses talked about God breaking off a branch from the top of a tree and planting it on a high *mountain* (Ezekiel 17:22). Similarly, they felt God had taken them from the comfort they had enjoyed in the States and sent them off to the *mountains* of Haiti. They talked of how painful leaving home was, like the breaking of a branch.

The verses went on to talk about the splendid fruit the new tree would bring and how many different kinds of birds would nest in it (Ezekiel 17:23). So they felt God had brought great success to their ministry in the mountains of Haiti and that many people had come to God as a result. Finally, the verses talked about how God dries up green trees and makes dry trees flourish (17:24). The couple wasn't quite sure what that might mean for them, but they were sure it was going to be wonderful.

Many Christians use the words of the Bible in this way. They read it believing that God speaks to them directly from the words with messages individually tailored for them. Some of these messages tell them what God wants them to do. I know of a family trying to decide whether to move to

Florida. At about the same time, three different family members had verses "speak" to them. One passage was about going to a better country (Hebrews 11:14-16). Another was about submitting to God's will (Psalm 139). Finally, a daughter came upon a verse in Judges in which a woman says "thou hast given me a south land" (1:15, King James Version). The family believed God was leading them from Indiana to Florida.

Others hear verses telling them what is going to happen in the future. Perhaps you have a friend with cancer and come across Isaiah 53:5: "with his stripes we are healed" (KJV). The person might believe God was going to heal the cancer. A different person in this situation comes across Luke 2:29: "now lettest thou thy servant depart in peace" (KJV). Perhaps this person concludes his or her friend will not be healed.

I wouldn't tell such people that God didn't speak to them or that God doesn't speak in these ways. If you believe God spoke to Moses at a burning bush (Exodus 3) or to Balaam through a donkey (Numbers 22), why couldn't he make the words of the Bible "jump out" at people in highly personal and individualistic ways? If God speaks to ordinary people, why wouldn't he speak directly through the words of the Bible?

On the other hand, God could speak to people through *any* words in this way. He could make a phrase from a *Reader's Digest* jump out at you. You could hear a comment on a TV show or even see a road sign and hear God telling you something. In short, God could take words *out of any context* and make them come alive to you. Nevertheless, many Christians believe God speaks regularly through the Bible in this way. Christians often view the words of the Bible as somewhat "magical" words designed to take on hidden meanings.

But of course none of these meanings are the meanings these words had *originally* when they were

> Many Christians treat the words of the Bible as somewhat "magical" words designed to take on hidden meanings.

first spoken and written down. Such meanings are not, for example, what Jesus had in mind when he spoke to the multitudes. As we saw in the Introduction, words are highly flexible things. Interpretations like these are highly personalized and individualistic. They take place when someone brings the highly specific "dictionary" of his or her life to the words of the text.

Christians who read the Bible in this way are not reading its words "in context." They are investing meanings in the words *from their own context*, giving them new meanings that those words have never had before. At best, these are instances of God inspiring the words to *become* the words of God to an individual—God meeting someone by way of his or her "personal dictionary."

> At best these are instances of God inspiring the words to become the words of God to an individual. But these meanings are not what the words originally meant.

The missionaries who heard God's voice in Ezekiel 17 may indeed have heard God's voice. But their interpretation had almost nothing to do with anything God might have revealed to the ancient nation of Israel 2500 years ago. Ezekiel's prophecy dealt specifically with events surrounding the reign of a king named Zedekiah, king of a nation called Judah, in around the year 591BC. Someone who reads these verses in terms of today may be hearing God, but he or she is not reading the words for what they really meant. The case is the same for the other examples we gave at the beginning of the chapter.

Bad Impressions

Here we encounter a potential problem. This way of reading the Bible no doubt works fine if you are genuinely hearing God in the words. Such a meaning would then be inspired and fully authoritative. On the other hand, the words of the Bible can come to mean *anything* using this method. What happens when a person is *not* genuinely hearing God in the words?

I heard a story once of three young college students who all believed God had told them to marry the same girl. Perhaps they all believed they had heard God's voice in some verse (e.g., Psalm 37:4 in the KJV: "he shall give thee the desires of thine heart"). The woman did not marry any of them. What happens when different individuals hear contradictory messages in the same words? What happens when you are the only one who hears the message?

"Spiritual" interpretations like these are only legitimate if God is actually behind them. In other words, their legitimacy does not really come from the words of the Bible itself, but from God speaking through them. People have made any number of inappropriate, even devilish interpretations of the Bible's words throughout the centuries. They have committed murders, divorced spouses, even attempted genocide using the Bible's words as justification. Clearly the authority of the Bible's words is only as legitimate as the dictionary you bring to the words.

Perhaps you have heard of trying to find God's will by the "hunt and peck" method. You open the

> The authority of the Bible's words is only as legitimate as the dictionary you bring to the words.

Bible up at random and point to a verse to get a message from God. There is a story about someone who did this and opened to Matthew 27:5, where Judas "departed, and went and hanged himself" (KJV). A bit disturbed, the man tried again, this time flipping to Luke 10:37, "Go, and do thou likewise" (KJV). Now desperate, he turned to John 13:27, "That thou doest, do quickly" (KJV).

Of course none of these verses originally had anything to do with this hypothetical Christian. And if this situation ever happened to someone, most would have enough sense not to commit suicide. Nevertheless it is a good illustration of the dangers involved in reading the Bible's words out of context.

In the end, using the Bible in these kinds of ways provides a subtle way for the crazy, the power hungry, and even the well-intentioned to mistake their own thoughts for those of God. You may remember a man named David Koresh. This man believed that the Bible was without any error and that it had absolute authority when it was interpreted correctly.

On the other hand, he did not read its words in context. Isaiah 45:1 refers to a man named Cyrus as the LORD's "anointed one."[2] David Koresh thought the verse was about himself. He took the Hebrew word for Cyrus (Koresh), added the word to his name, and saw himself as the messiah.[3] Of course the verse was originally about the Persian king Cyrus who permitted the Jews to return to Jerusalem from Babylon in 538BC.

We could recount story after story of similar situations in which an unbalanced person committed some atrocious act, using the words of the Bible as their justification. Mothers have killed their children. Husbands have justified affairs. People have shot abortion doctors, lynched African-Americans, and dragged homosexuals to their death in the name of God and the Bible. The Bible is a very dangerous tool in the hands of such people, because it is easy to make the words say what you want them to say.

> The Bible is a dangerous tool in the hands of some individuals, because it is easy to make the words say what you want them to say.

The Bible has an abundant supply of verses a person might use to justify evil thoughts or actions. What might a lunatic do with Psalm 137:8-9? These verses applaud anyone who would dash a Babylonian infant against a rock. God commanded Joshua to obliterate all Canaanites—men, women, children, even animals (e.g., Joshua 6:21). Did some medieval crusaders see in these verses a command to kill all Muslims for Christ?

Deuteronomy 21:21 says that a stubborn and rebellious son must be put to death. Deuteronomy 22:22 says that a couple found committing adultery is to die. No doubt more than one person has killed their children or spouse using these verses as justification. Ezra 10:3 is about Ezra's command for Israelites to divorce their foreign-born wives and to put away the children from those marriages. Some colleges take these words out of context and forbid interracial dating among their students. I can see someone using them as an excuse to divorce their spouse and not pay child support. There is no limit to what someone can do with these words once they are loosed from their context.

Others use the Bible, often unknowingly, to boost their sense of self-worth or to attain a level of leadership they would not otherwise be able to obtain. A person with few life experiences, ability, or intellect can speak with the authority and certainty of God if he or she has a Bible in hand. Many Christian groups have a decidedly anti-intellectual edge that actually applauds irrationality and resists those who might go to college or seminary to study the Bible.

No doubt God can and does speak powerfully through individuals like Billy Sunday, who had little formal education. But all interpretations of Scripture are subject to scrutiny by other Christians, no matter how inspired someone may claim to be. As Paul wrote, "the spirits of prophets are subject to prophets" (1 Corinthians 14:32). The interpretations of such individuals must be tested by the church, not blindly accepted.

An individual with charisma can escape common-sense scrutiny when he or she has a Bible in hand. While Jim Jones did not have a high respect for the Bible, he is a good example of how a megalomaniac can use religion to by-pass basic common sense. As you may remember, he led his congregation to Guyana and forced them to commit mass suicide. You can imagine the power a charismatic individual can weal with a Bible in his or her hand.

When we allow individuals to decide what the Bible means, the Bible can play into the hands of all our psychological quirks and problems. The strong possibility of bad impressions makes it clear that "spiritual readings" of the Bible are safest in large groups of Christians who can test and prove them. We can only regret that such a broader group did not convince David Koresh that his revelations had nothing to do with God, let alone the true meaning of Isaiah 45. The potential for spiritual misinterpretation pushes us to read the Bible in communities where other Christians can help us keep things in perspective.

Prophets Among Us?

But we should perhaps also allow for the possibility of authentic prophetic voices among us. Prophets are usually not popular individuals. Their own people frequently give them the hardest time (e.g., Matthew 13:57). It is often only in hindsight, perhaps even long after the prophet is dead, that the trueness of his or her words becomes clear.

But does God inspire "prophetic" interpretations of Scripture that have little or nothing to do with what the Bible actually meant when it was first written? The New Testament itself thrusts this question on us because it regularly reads the Old Testament out of context to one degree or another. To put it another way, the New Testament frequently reads the words of the Old Testament against the context of its own day rather than in terms of its original context. In particular, it often reads the words of the Old Testament in terms of Christ.

For example, the Gospel of Matthew is notorious for the way it regularly reads the Old Testament in ways never imagined by the Old

> The New Testament frequently reads the words of the Old Testament out of context to one degree or another. It often reads the words in terms of Christ.

Testament authors. It sees various events in the life of Christ as "fulfillments" of prophecy. But these are usually "prophecies" hidden in the words, not straightforward predictions that come to pass in the life of Christ. In other words, Matthew finds various phrases or statements of the Old Testament that he applies to Jesus out of context—they did not originally refer to Jesus. Perhaps God inspired Matthew to read Scripture in this way, but he was clearly following the interpretive methods of his day rather than the way we try to read things for what they really meant.

One example is when Matthew tells us that Jesus and his parents went down to Egypt for a short time. Matthew says that their later departure from Egypt happened "to fulfill what was spoken by the Lord through the prophet, saying, 'Out of Egypt I called my son'" (Matthew 2:15). Since Matthew is quoting the Old Testament prophet Hosea, we expect to turn to Hosea 11:1-2 and find a prediction that the messiah would leave Egypt at some point in his life.

However, when we turn to Hosea 11:1-2, we find the following words: "When *Israel* was a child, I loved him, and *out of Egypt I called my son*. While I called to them, they walked from my face. To the Baals they sacrificed and to idols they offered incense." Many of us are shocked. We expected the Old Testament to predict something about Jesus the messiah.

But this verse had nothing to do with Jesus originally; it was about the nation Israel. And it wasn't about the future; it was about the past—in fact an event that happened hundreds of years before Hosea himself, let alone before Jesus. Hosea was writing about the exodus of Israel from Egypt. The verses go on to talk about how Israel, God's "son," consistently turned away from God to worship other gods. No Christian could believe that this verse was originally about Jesus!

There is no reason to be troubled at these observations, although we may have to rethink what the New Testament is doing when it speaks of fulfilled prophecy. Like most Jews then and many Christians today, Matthew wasn't reading the Old Testament in context. Matthew found the words "out of Egypt I called my son" in Hosea. These words reminded him of something that took place in the life of Jesus. It didn't matter that the words had nothing to do with Jesus in their original context.[4]

If we do a careful study of the other points at which the New Testament quotes the Old, we will find the same phenomenon over and over again to varying degrees. Sometimes the New Testament pays more attention to the original context than others. This fact creates an inner conflict for those who say that the literal meaning of the Bible is the only authoritative meaning for us. After all, when we interpret the Bible literally, we find that the Bible usually does not interpret itself literally.

Christians have dealt with this phenomenon in different ways. I have heard some Bible professors say that Matthew could interpret this way because he was inspired. You don't have that luxury. Catholics of the early twentieth century invoked an idea they called *sensus plenior* or a "fuller sense" to try to give the words of Scripture both a valid literal meaning and an inspired, valid second meaning. The original meaning was that of the Old Testament author, the fuller sense the meaning the New Testament authors saw through the eyes of the Spirit.

> The way the New Testament itself interprets the Old creates an inner conflict for those who say the literal meaning of the Bible is the only authoritative meaning for us. When we interpret the Bible literally, we find that the Bible does not interpret itself literally.

For example, many Christians are well acquainted with Isaiah 7:14: "The virgin will be with child and will give birth to a son, and will call him Immanuel" (New International Version). Matthew 1:23 understands this verse in Isaiah as a prophecy about Jesus' birth by way of the Virgin Mary. We expect to turn to Isaiah and find a verse about the future messiah's birth.

For this reason you can understand why many Christians were outraged when the Revised Standard Version of the Bible came out in the 1950's. Its translation of Isaiah 7:14 read, "A *young woman* will conceive." Many Christians thought the RSV translators didn't believe in the virgin birth.

But when we read Isaiah in context, we find that the RSV was simply translating the words for what they meant *originally*, rather than in the "spiritual" way Matthew understood them. In the original context of Isaiah, these verses were a promise from God to a king named Ahaz. Ahaz was worried about two neighboring kings who were threatening to destroy his kingdom. The prophet Isaiah offered Ahaz a sign that they wouldn't defeat him. A young woman (the most natural meaning of the Hebrew word *'alma*) would give birth to a son, and "before the boy knows enough to reject the wrong and choose the right, the land of the two kings you dread will be laid waste" (Isaiah 7:16, NIV).

Now if this passage were originally about Jesus, then the sign was of no value to Ahaz. After all, Ahaz had been dead for some 700 years before Jesus came to earth. If the child wasn't someone Ahaz himself knew, then it was no sign to him. The prophecy must have originally referred to a child born very soon after Isaiah made the prophecy, probably an heir to Ahaz's throne.[5]

Those who believe in a "fuller sense" to Scripture would argue that both meanings are correct: both the original meaning and the fuller sense Matthew saw. Some would suggest that God "hid" this second meaning in the words so that it would jump out at the earliest Christians about Jesus. Indeed, for whatever reason, those who translated the Old Testament from Hebrew into Greek about 250 years before Christ used a word that really did mean "virgin" and *not* primarily "young woman." You could argue that God inspired their translation so that the Scripture was set up to point to the virgin birth of Christ when he arrived on earth.[6]

You might even suggest that some verses have even more than two inspired meanings. For example,

> Some would suggest that God hid countless meanings in the words of Scripture just waiting to jump out at Christians at various times and places.

Daniel 11:31 talks about how a certain "king from the north" would desecrate the Jewish temple in Jerusalem. This event took place in the year 175BC, when a king to the north of Israel set up a statue to Zeus in the Jerusalem temple and desecrated it. The events of Daniel 11 read like a history book on the reign of this king, Antiochus Epiphanes IV.

We find this same imagery in Mark 13:14 as Jesus talks about the destruction and desecration of Jerusalem that took place in AD70 (see Luke 21:20). And some Christian teachers also think these verses refer to events that will take place in Jerusalem in the days yet to come. Are there countless verses that God planted in Scripture knowing that they would jump out *at you and me* 2000 years later? I wouldn't deny this possibility.

But all these "prophetic" meanings are different from the original meanings. It is possible that they are inspired, but they are not what these texts really meant originally. Much of modern prophecy teaching takes the words of the Bible out of context on a massive scale. Most of the verses "prophecy teachers" use were originally about ancient events that have long since taken place and have little or nothing to do with today. But it is at least possible that those who see these meanings are modern day prophets, individuals God has inspired to see the future in the words of the Bible. We'll know for sure if their predictions come true.

Did God impregnate the words of Scripture with incredibly complex networks of inspiration set to speak to millions of different individuals in millions of different ways? If God is God, it is certainly possible. Then again, words are flexible enough for God to inspire meanings like these on the spot as we read. And words are certainly flexible enough for countless individuals to find uninspired meanings in the text!

Are there prophets among us who hear God's word by way of intensely personal readings of Scripture out of context? I will not say there are not. Can God make random words of the Bible come alive in a way that speaks to you? I will not say he does not. But we must keep in mind that this "magical" use of the words will usually have nothing to do with what the words really meant when they first found their way to the earth.

Devotions with Open Eyes

I found great comfort as a child from verses like Joshua 1:9: "Be strong and of a good courage; be not afraid, neither be thou dismayed, for the LORD thy God is with thee whithersoever thou goest" (KJV). Another one was Jeremiah 29:11: "For I know the thoughts that I think toward you, saith the LORD, thoughts of peace, and not of evil" (KJV). I found peace in the idea that God was with me wherever I went and that God was looking out for my benefit, not to harm me.

When I read these verses in context today, I realize that neither of them was originally directed at me or anyone alive today. Joshua 1:9 was a promise *to Joshua* as he was about to launch a military campaign to take over the Promised Land.[7] God encouraged Joshua in this task, telling him to have courage. God promised that he would go with Joshua wherever he went. In other words, God gave Joshua victory over his enemies and made him a successful leader.

Why did I think this verse was about me? Could others read this verse as a message to them? Would this verse have applied to Hitler as he was about to invade Austria or Poland?

Jeremiah 29:11 was a promise God sent by way of the prophet Jeremiah *to captive Israelites in Babylon*. The message was that God was not done with them—one day God would bring them back from Babylon to Jerusalem, a promise that took place in 538BC. Why did I think this verse was about me? Could anyone apply this verse to him or herself? Does God always plan to deliver those in perilous circumstances, even those who are not serving him?

These simple examples show how programmed we are to read the words of the Bible out of context. If I had paid even a little attention to the verses that came before and after Joshua 1:9 and Jeremiah 29:11, I could have easily seen that these verses were not originally about me at all. They were about specific situations in the lives of Joshua and Jeremiah. As obvious as this fact is, I was not taught to read the words of the Bible for what they really meant when they were written. I was programmed to read them as direct words from God to me.

But these facts do not negate the truths I took from these verses. God does love me and have good plans for me ultimately. But the truth of my conclusions did not ultimately come from the verses I was reading. It came more from a set of Christian beliefs I brought with me to the text, beliefs I was taught growing up in church.

We inherit "guidelines of faith" like these from the Christian traditions around us, rules for the kinds of meanings we "are allowed" to see in the words of Scripture.[8] Ideally the original meaning of the Bible would have something to do with these "guidelines." But we more often than not appropriate the Bible's teaching in a filtered form, as processed by the Christian traditions around us. By the end of the book I will argue that we best make the common ground of Christianity throughout the ages as the main source of such "guidelines."

Far be it from me to tell anyone to stop hearing God's voice in the words of the Bible, whether what they are hearing has anything to do with the original meaning or not. Indeed, if we have to know the original meaning to hear God, then most Christians throughout the ages are in trouble. But the more we know about the original meaning and ourselves, the better equipped we are to have our "devotions" with our eyes open to what is going on. Surely the more truth we know, the better able we are to be in tune with God, who is the ultimate source of all truth.

The Bible has taken on a kind of "sacramental" quality, especially among Protestants. A sacrament is a means of experiencing God's grace.

> The Bible can take on a sacramental quality where it becomes a means of experiencing God's gracious revelation. Ordinary words are transformed into the voice of God.

In the case of baptism and communion, an ordinary substance like water, bread, or wine becomes a catalyst for experiencing cleansing or the presence of Christ. Words are also ordinary things. But when the Spirit chooses to speak through them, they become transformed into the voice of God. God seems to speak to many Christian individuals in this way through the words of the Bible.

---

[1] I don't remember the precise details of the story, but the ones I present here convey the point accurately.

[2] The Hebrew *meshiach*, a word that would come to mean "messiah."

[3] This information comes from Koresh's Video Bible Study, January 5, 1992

[4] Some scholars go to great lengths to find *some* aspect of the original context of verses like these to justify "fulfillments" like these. But such a struggle has everything to do with us and little to do with Matthew. It is our faulty paradigm for interpreting Scripture that causes our pain. Matthew was not pained by reading the Old Testament out of context. How can we find anything substantial about Judges 13:5 and 7 or Isaiah 11:1 or 53:2 to explain the fulfillment of Matthew 2:23 other than the fact that the word *branch* in Hebrew (*nazir*) bears some resemblance to the name of the city *Nazareth*?

5 The same concept applies to verses in Isaiah 9 implying that this child would be called "Mighty God," "Everlasting Father," and "Prince of Peace" (9:6-7). These verses were originally about a human king. To be sure, no Israelite confused the human king with Yahweh—the literal GOD. Yet we cannot pay attention to the words of the Old Testament in context without concluding that they could also use this language figuratively in reference to their human kings. For example, Psalm 45 is a psalm for the wedding of a human king (e.g. see 45:9-15). Yet this human king is addressed at one point in the psalm as "God" (45:6) in distinction from *the* GOD (45:7). Isaiah 9 was thus using divine language of its king, just as was the normal practice of the ancient near east.

6 Indeed, since most of us do not read the Bible in Greek, Hebrew, or Aramaic, we must suppose that God frequently speaks through the wording of translations even beyond the original words. New Testament authors occasionally made points from the way the Old Testament had been translated into Greek even when the original Hebrew did not support those points. Thus Hebrews 10:5 makes an argument from the word "body" in Psalm 40:6, even though this word was not in the original Hebrew of the verse.

7 By the end of the book we will see that the situation is far more complex than what I suggest here. The book of Joshua itself did not reach its "final" form until centuries after Joshua's death (e.g., it even relies on older books *about* Joshua, like the book of Jashar mentioned in Josh. 10:13). The book as a whole offered hope to Israel as God's people at this much later time. In that sense the "original meaning" of the verse probably *did* concern a much broader audience than an individual promise to Joshua—still an ancient one, however.

8 The idea of a "rule of faith" was a major category by which some of the earliest Christians determined what were appropriate beliefs and interpretations (e.g., Irenaeus in the late 100's). See F. Young, *The Art of Performance: Toward a Theology of Holy Scripture* (London: Darton, Longman, and Todd, 1990), 45-65.

Chapter 2
When Church Groups Decide

Denominational Glasses

A denomination is a collection of individual churches with some sort of common organization or belief. So while all Baptists have some things in common, there are a number of Baptist *denominations*: Southern Baptist, American Baptist, Primitive Baptist, Free Will Baptists, etc. Different groups like these usually have come from some common group at some point in the past and have "split"—sometimes more than once—because of some disagreement over belief or practice.

Some of these church contentions seem somewhat ridiculous in hindsight, like groups who have argued over the color of the bumper on their cars (Black Bumper Mennonites), not to mention those who thought it wrong to have a car in the first place (Amish). Groups have split over whether you should use instruments in the church (Christian Church) or whether a person should be baptized forward or backward, certainly by immersion. Hair length and jewelry have played their role, even whether you had to lease your seat in the church (*Free* Methodist).

Groups like these usually have highly developed "dictionaries" that they use when they are reading the Bible. When a Baptist brings a Baptist "dictionary" to the Bible, we shouldn't be surprised if s/he "finds" Baptist meanings. The same is true of a Catholic, Methodist, or Lutheran.[1] We all have a tendency to focus on verses that our tradition has selected and defined in our favor.

This process does not always take place consciously. For example, the Methodist tradition lays almost no emphasis on the idea of predestination—the idea that God has already decided who will become a Christian and arranged their destinies accordingly. Instead, this tradition tends to emphasize that anyone can become a Christian of his or her own free will. The result is that Methodists generally read right past the many places in the New Testament where the Bible uses language of "calling" and "election" (e.g., 1 Corinthians 1:2). It is not necessarily anyone's intention to ignore such verses; they just don't come up on a Methodist's radar screen. On the other hand, a good Presbyterian will pick up on this language every time.

We see the dictionaries of various groups constantly at work as they read the Bible. For example, someone from the United Pentecostal Church will probably hear overtones of speaking in tongues every time the New Testament refers to a Christian having the Holy Spirit. This church believes that speaking in "spiritual" languages is a sign of having God's Spirit within you, something that all true Christians demonstrate. So while the vast majority of instances where the Holy Spirit is mentioned in the Bible do *not* mention tongues, someone from the UPC will infer that tongues is always implied.

I myself was raised in a church that in part grew out of the "holiness revivals" of the late nineteenth century.[2] This movement emphasized an experience a Christian could and should have at some point after being a Christian. This experience, called "entire sanctification," involved the removal or successful suppression of the part of you that makes you want to sin. The result was a life in which a person became "perfect" in love and at least potentially sinless in intent for the rest of his or her life.

When I was a teenager, I read through the Bible and highlighted in orange all the verses I came across that mentioned words like "holiness," "holy," "sanctification," etc. Using my holiness "dictionary," all references of this kind immediately triggered in my mind the full blown doctrine of entire sanctification taught by my church.[3] Then as I worked my way through college and seminary, I began to look for a place where this understanding of sanctification was clearly spelled out. I slowly realized that there was no one place where the Bible laid out this doctrine in the form I had learned it. Rather my tradition had pieced its teaching together from various items found here and there. In other words, I could only find the full blown doctrine in a text if I came to it with my church's definition of holiness and sanctification already in hand.

It is of course always easier to see the "denominational glasses" of other groups, the idiosyncratic beliefs that color the interpretations of denominations other than our own. It is much harder to see our own glasses and biases. A Lutheran can see more easily than a Baptist that the New Testament never engages in any debate over the way a person is baptized. A Catholic can see more easily than a Lutheran that Paul affirmed the importance of good works in the life of a Christian. And a Protestant can see more easily than a Catholic that Mary most likely went on to have other children after Jesus was born.

One factor that complicates matters is that you can almost always find some verse that at least sounds like it supports your position. Even those Protestants who first argued so strongly that the Bible's meaning is clear[4] also recognized that some passages are more difficult to understand than others. They believed the message was clear with regard to "everything necessary for salvation." When we find something that is unclear, they believed we should use the "clear" verses to interpret the "unclear" ones: "Scripture interprets Scripture."

The very real practical problem with this approach is of course to figure out which verses are the "clear"

> You can almost always find some verse that at least sounds like it supports your church's position.

ones and which ones are the "unclear" ones. The history of Protestantism especially shows that Christian groups frequently disagree on which is which. For example, take the question of whether women should be ministers or not. It would be wrong to assume that everyone who believes that the Bible is without error will oppose women in ministry. There are any number of very conservative Christian groups who have female ministers.[5]

Those who oppose women in ministry consider the teaching of 1 Corinthians 14:34-35 and 1 Timothy 2:12-15 to be the "clear" teaching.

Corinthians says "women should be silent in the churches. For they are not permitted to speak, but should be subordinate, as the law also says" (1 Corinthians 14:34). Timothy says, "I permit no woman to teach or to have authority over a man; she is to keep silent" (1 Timothy 2:12). What could be clearer teaching than we have here, the Southern Baptist says.

But what do we make of Acts 2:17, says the Wesleyan: "[Y]our sons *and daughters* shall prophesy." What of the spiritual principle of Galatians 3:28: "there is no longer male and female; for all of you are one in Christ Jesus"? What of the fact that we see Priscilla instructing Apollos in Acts 18:26 and Phoebe having a prominent role in the church of Cenchrea (Romans 16:10). Junia may actually have been a second order apostle (Romans 16:7)? The verses you consider to be "clear" will usually turn out to be the ones that most benefit the position of your group.

The issue of homosexuality makes this point in an emphatic way. Most Christian groups assume that verses like Leviticus 18:22; 20:13; Romans 1:26-27; 1 Corinthians 6:9; and 1 Timothy 1:10 make it overwhelmingly clear that the Bible is opposed to the practice of homosexual sex. But a visit to the website of the Metropolitan Community Church makes it clear that 1) there are practicing homosexuals who believe that the Bible is authoritative and 2) these individuals do not believe that the verses above address a monogamous homosexual relationship.

Some of the reasons for such disagreements should be fairly clear by now. While it is possible that such disagreements sometimes come from spiritual problems, a more basic cause is the potential ambiguity of words. Words without a clear context are highly flexible in their meaning. The context we bring to them, the "dictionary" we bring to the words, completely and utterly determines the meaning we find in them. We can almost always find some words in Scripture that come out the way we want them to when we are using the dictionary of our church group.

But even when we come to the words with our own dictionary, we also will almost always find verses that don't sound the way I want them to. No one's dictionary is completely made up of idiosyncratic meanings—I absorb a great deal of my dictionary from my broader culture. I call verses that don't fit as neatly into my religious viewpoint "naughty" verses.

Almost every way of looking at the world has some "kinks" to work out, problem data that doesn't fit neatly into my viewpoint. Science works this way. Almost every scientific paradigm or theory has problems that scientists are trying to work out.[6] It is usually only after repeated attempts to account for a certain problem, to explain some "naughty data" that doesn't fit the paradigm, that another scientist, often a younger one, might begin to wonder whether a new theory needs to be developed.

Even then such a scientist often faces strong opposition from the majority who still favor the prevailing theory. Such a person may have difficulty getting his or her work published at first. It is only if the new theory gains momentum—and of course the other scientists die off—that a scientific revolution is ensured success.

> There will always be verses that at least sound like they are in tension with the positions of your group, "naughty" verses. Such verses are deemphasized and redefined so that they do not interfere with the group's overall "paradigm," its way of processing the world.

The ideological frameworks by which we process the Bible's teaching function similarly to scientific paradigms. Our perspectives on religious truth are persistent and generally resist change. The natural tendency is to ignore the "naughty data" and focus primarily on the words that come to have the meanings most favorable to our thinking when we bring our "dictionary" to bear on them. Almost inevitably, these "clear" passages are the ones you will hear preached regularly from the pulpits of the denomination. The person in the pew may not even be aware of the naughty ones.

Of course other processes are also at work. From time to time someone will focus on the "naughty data" in one way or another. Such a person may work to reform the denomination or, if unsuccessful, may leave it. If the person has simply brought his or her own idiosyncratic "dictionary" to the text, he or she may form a new group. Such a group will tend to be sectarian and divisive in nature, sometimes even cultish.

On the other hand, if the naughty data exposes what are already idiosyncratic views of the denomination, the person may leave the church for a more mainstream group. Unless the group as a whole has been moving in the same direction, such individuals are bound to face strong opposition from the group, perhaps even "de-Christianization." On the whole, groups tend to become more mainstream over time, often considered a "liberalization" of the denomination. At some point in that process we will often find smaller groups splitting off of the parent group. These groups usually wish to retain or recapture the denomination's original teaching and fervor, to return to the group's earlier "dictionary."

Different Books, Different Contexts

We have described some of the dynamics involved in how churches "select" and "deselect" various verses in Scripture as an expression of their identity. Perhaps every church group has favorite verses that they define in a way that reinforces who they are. At the same time there will always be verses that at least sound like they are in tension with the positions of the group, "naughty" verses. Such verses are deemphasized and redefined so that they do not interfere with the group's overall "paradigm," their way of processing the world.

One factor that aggravates the problem is the fact that the Bible is made up of so many different books from so many different contexts. In contrast, many Christians and Christian groups interpret the Bible as if it were a single book. True, the Bible looks like a single book when I buy it at the bookstore today. But it was not a single book originally. The Bible is actually a collection of dozens of books that only began

> The Bible is more like a library of books than a single book.

to circulate together as a whole hundreds of years after they were first written.[7] When I look at the Bible, I am looking at a library of books rather than a single one. Most Protestant Bibles have sixty-six books in them. Roman Catholic Bibles have several others, and Orthodox Bibles even more.

The material in these books came into existence over a period of as much as a thousand years. These books were written in three different languages in several different regions of the ancient world. Each book used words in the same ways that its specific author and audience used them—otherwise the message wouldn't have made any sense to those for whom these books were actually written. When I view the Bible as a single book, *my* context becomes the unifying context for the words. Perhaps inadvertently, I lift the words out of their specific and diverse original contexts and read them in terms of my unified one.

For example, many Christians interpret Revelation 22:18-19 as a warning not to add or take away anything from the Bible: "I witness to everyone who hears the words of the prophecy of this book: if someone should add to them, God will add to that person the plagues written in this book. And if someone takes away from the words of the book of this prophecy, God will take away that person's part from the tree of life and from the holy city, which are written in this book."

Since these words come at the end of the Bible as it is currently "packaged," it is only natural that many Christians take it as a reference to the whole Bible. After all, it comes in the last chapter. Many interpret these verses to mean that anyone who adds to the Bible will be cursed while anyone who takes away from the Bible will lose their reward.

> Reading the Bible as a single book leads us to read it consistently out of context.

But now we reflect that Revelation was first written as a self-contained book on an individual scroll. Indeed, Christians did not universally agree that it should even be considered Scripture until the 300's and 400's. Clearly these two verses originally referred only to the book of Revelation itself. Perhaps we can apply the statement to the other books of the Bible as well. But once we make this move, we have loosed the meaning from its mooring and allowed the text to take on meanings beyond the literal.

2 Timothy 3:16 is often quoted as the Bible's claim to be inspired: "All Scripture is given by inspiration of God, and is profitable for doctrine, for reproof, for correction, for instruction in righteousness" (KJV). Psalm 119:105 similarly says, "Your word is a lamp for my feet and a light for my path." Both these verses are regularly taken in reference to the entire Bible.

Perhaps it appropriate for Christians to read these verses in this way. But at the same time notice the subtle way in which we have changed the meanings of these verses from what they originally meant. The Scriptures that Timothy would have learned from his infancy were the Old Testament, not the whole Bible. Some of the books of the New Testament certainly existed at the time of 2 Timothy, but they were not the Scriptures in view here. In context, 2 Timothy referred to the Jewish Scriptures, which Christians call the "Old Testament."

Psalm 119:105 similarly referred originally to the Pentateuch or Jewish law: Genesis, Exodus, Leviticus, Numbers, and Deuteronomy. Surely the whole Bible is a light for us, but this was not the original meaning of the psalm. Not a single book of the New Testament was written at the time of this psalm. By reading the verse in the light of the whole Bible we have created a new meaning for the verse. We have changed the definition of God's "word" by changing the context against which we read the verse.

We could produce countless examples of Christians introducing concepts from one part of the Bible into another, ideas we would not otherwise see in the verses themselves. On the one hand, it is not clear to me that reading the Bible this way is ultimately a bad thing. After all, this process reflects the idea that "Scripture interprets Scripture," an idea that historically has been used by both

Protestants and Catholics alike.[8] It is the way that most Christians have read the Bible throughout the ages to one degree or another.

But at the same time it is clear that this practice results in interpretations that are different from what these books actually meant originally. In other words, we read the Bible in this way at the expense of hearing accurately what Paul really meant—or Matthew or Isaiah. When you change the context and definitions of the words, you change the way they are used and thus you change the meaning of the words.

We should not be surprised to find that different books of the Bible use words differently. Even within the United States we find regional terms and phrases, like whether you drink "pop," "soda," or "a Coke"—even when it isn't a Coke. Do you use a "vacuum," a "sweeper," or if you are in England, a "Hoover"? Even individuals have their favorite expressions and ways of talking about things, the kinds of things our friends say when they are imitating us.

Now consider that David lived a thousand years before Christ in the Late Bronze Age and composed psalms just after Israel became a unified kingdom for the first time. Ezekiel lived in captivity in Babylon over five hundred years before Christ hundreds of miles east of a destroyed Jerusalem. Paul wrote in the Greek and Latin-speaking cities of Greece and ancient Turkey in the first century after Christ. And Matthew was probably written in northern Syria even later still after Jerusalem had been destroyed again. We should not expect these individuals to use words in the same ways since they wrote in vastly different settings and wrote for vastly different audiences.

If we think these individuals all used words the same ways and had common meanings, we are not reading them in context. We are creating a unity of meaning by placing all their words into *our* theological context. This diversity is not a negative feature of the Bible, and it does not discount the significance of these books in any way. After all, why wouldn't God have spoken in the categories of the people he was actually speaking to? It is a subtle narcissism to think that the meanings of the individual books of the Bible have to fit easily with one another from my perspective. I am not the original audience of any of these books—they were.

An awareness of this diversity actually makes it easier to account for some "naughty data" in the text by taking individual contexts into

> It is a subtle narcissism to think that the meanings of the individual books of the Bible have to fit easily with one another from my perspective.

account. For example, we face a hopeless contradiction between Mark and John if we think they both use their words in exactly the same way. Jesus says in Mark 8:12 that he will not give any signs (*sēmeia*) at all to his audience. But John 20:30-31 says that Jesus gave many signs (*sēmeia*), even more than recorded. Clearly Mark and John use the word *sign* differently.

James 2:24 says that individuals are considered right with God on the basis of their works (*erga*) and not by faith (*pistis*) alone. Ephesians 2:8-9 says that Christians are saved through faith (*pistis*) and not by works (*erga*). Either the words are being used with slightly different meanings or these two authors disagree with one another.

It is crucial to observe that the process of integrating these seemingly conflicting passages into a unified meaning is a process that takes place *outside* the biblical text itself. The individual books of the Bible themselves almost never tell us how to connect their teaching with the teachings of the other books. In other words, the final step of integration, the most important step in determining "what the Bible means" as a whole, is one that the Bible itself does not tell us how to take!

> The final step of integrating the Bible's diverse teaching, the most important step in deciding what the Bible means as a whole, is one that the Bible itself does not tell us how to take.

The main exception would be the way the way New Testament interprets the Old, for the books of the New Testament do frequently point to ways we can integrate their words with those of various parts of the Old Testament. For example, we saw in the last chapter that the literal meaning of the Old Testament was frequently tangential for the

New Testament authors. In other words, the New Testament implies that one way to integrate its teaching with the Old Testament is to place the words of the Old Testament into the context of Christian revelation.

Here is a testimony to the flexibility of words. In context, the words of the Old Testament are the Jewish Bible, the Hebrew Scriptures.

> Placed within the context of the "New" Testament, the words of the Jewish Bible become the "Old" Testament and take on new meanings in their new context.

But placed within the context of the "New" Testament, they become the "Old" Testament, and the same words take on new meanings in their new context. You might be surprised at how differently a non-Christian Jew reads these words from how your typical Christian does.

But even within the New Testament we find diversity in how to appropriate the Old Testament, particularly its ethical teaching. Thus Matthew tells us that Jesus did *not* come to destroy the law (Matt. 5:17). True, Matthew's Jesus transforms it by making love the ultimate principle for filtering it. The rules on murder and adultery become stricter—it becomes wrong even to contemplate such things (Matthew 5:21-30). Jesus prohibits divorce (Matthew 5:31-32), although the Old Testament allowed it freely (Deuteronomy 24:1) and even commanded it at points (Ezra 10:3). On the other hand, Jesus reverses the Old Testament law of retribution, "an eye for an eye," even though it is an Old Testament command (Matthew 5:38-42).[9] It becomes wrong to keep the law on this one.

But in contrast to Matthew, books like Mark, the letters of Paul, and the book of Hebrews all explicitly emphasize discontinuity with the Jewish law. If Matthew says that Jesus did *not* come to destroy the law, Ephesians says that Christ *has* abolished the law (Ephesians 2:15). Paul says he is not "under law" (1 Corinthians 9:20), and Mark says that Jesus declared all foods clean (Mark 7:19). The volume of scholarly books that attempt just to understand Paul's view of the Jewish law alone testifies to how difficult it can be to find a coherent biblical teaching on issues like these.

This process of connection, prioritization, selection, and de-selection ultimately takes place outside the biblical text. In the end, there are so many possible ways to fit the Bible's teaching together that it is no wonder we find so many differing positions on issues. The final step of deciding what "the Bible" means is a step that the Bible itself cannot take. We are the ones forced to integrate its varied teachings together.

Denominations and the Body of Christ

At some point we must wonder whether an insistence on the unity of the biblical text is the last vestige of a drive to read the Bible as a single text from God to us rather than as multiple texts inspired through human authors to ancient audiences. Is it the pretense that we form our understandings on the basis of the Bible alone that keeps us insisting on a unified meaning on some level? In other words, if the Bible alone is the source of truth, then we need to be able to find a "final answer" on each issue from the Bible.

Some find such unity by insisting that the same timeless principles run across the entire Scripture even if those truths play themselves out in individual books in time-bound ways. Thus perhaps each individual book is an example of God revealing a completely inspired and authoritative word without error to a specific context. But since these contexts differ from one another, we face the task of teasing the specific situational and cultural factors out from the more universal and timeless principles. Perhaps this is the correct strategy.

> Is it possible that God is so big and beyond our understanding that "he" can only be brought within our view by irreconcilable paradoxes and metaphors?

Or is it possible that God is so big and beyond our understanding that "he" can only be brought within our view by irreconcilable paradoxes?[10] Is it only in the middle of contradictory snapshots and kaleidoscopic flashes that we can even come close to capturing some sense of God's greatness, power, and truth? Do we ultimately need Matthew and Paul *not* to fit neatly together to catch a glimpse of the ultimate reality?

We wonder if the same is true to some extent with regard to the conflicting positions of the various denominations of Christendom. The Christian philosopher often feels obliged to resolve the question of whether God decides who will be saved (predestination) or whether we have the freedom to choose ourselves (free will). On a human plane, the two concepts contradict each other.

But who can speak for God? The Scriptures seem to affirm both as equally important truths. Who can say whether these two contradictory principles can exist paradoxically alongside one another in God? Perhaps this allowance for paradox is a potential strength of having church traditions that over-emphasize one teaching or another. Perhaps the human mind is not really capable of affirming paradoxical truths without blurring the concepts and watering down one truth or the other.

Maybe some of the diversity among different denominations is a help to the limitations of our human

> Maybe some of the diversity among different denominations is a help to the limitations of our human understanding.

understanding. Like the imagery of a body that the apostle Paul drew on (1 Corinthians 12), perhaps some denominations are the hands, others the feet— some the security of the believer in Christ and others the need for continued faithfulness; some the grace of God and others the need for good works. As a whole we make up one body, but we are different and distinct.

> We lose something when we force the meanings of individual books together, frequently creating a meaning that *none* of the books had.

Perhaps such an allowance for paradox might also let the books of the Bible hang in tension with each other at times, letting apparent conflict stand without always trying to resolve it. Perhaps we should let Matthew or James appear to disagree with Paul, if that is what they seem to do. We lose something when we force the meanings together, frequently creating a meaning that *none* of the books had.

[1] Some groups of course do not claim to get all their views from the Bible. To some extent, such groups are less concerned for the Bible to "mean" what they believe.

[2] The Wesleyan Church.

[3] In all fairness, the actual teaching of my denomination had more subtlety to it than the simple apprehension of my teenage mind.

[4] The doctrine of the so-called "perspicuity" of Scripture's meaning.

[5] E.g., small holiness and Pentecostal groups, as well as evangelical groups like the Free Methodist, Wesleyan, and Nazarene churches.

[6] See Thomas Kuhn, *The Structure of Scientific Revolutions*, 3rd ed. (Chicago: University of Chicago, 1996).

[7] The very word *Bible* comes from the Latin *biblia*, which means "little books"—books plural, not singular.

[8] The main difference is that Protestants have usually claimed to practice it without recourse to traditions outside of Scripture, while Catholics have practiced it while acknowledging the authority of Christian tradition as well.

[9] It is popular to interpret the Old Testament "eye for an eye" rule as a limitation of punishment rather than an insistence on it (in other words, you cannot take two eyes for one). No doubt there is some truth to this approach. But this line of interpretation also seems to reflect our own cultural glasses and the subtle reinterpretation of the words we do so often to keep the words of the Bible from becoming too foreign to us. The preface to Deut. 19:21— "show no pity"—makes it clear that the law was insisting on equal retribution. If there is any distinction, it is that the law of Deuteronomy is "governmental" while Jesus' teaching is aimed at the individual.

[10] Even referring to God as "he" is an example of a metaphor, for God clearly has no literal male genitalia.

Chapter 3
When Cultures Decide

Cultural Assumptions

The last few decades have seen an explosion of Bible translations: The New International Version, The New Living Translation, The Message, The New Revised Standard Version, The English Standard Version, etc. The multiplicity of versions is sometimes as confusing as the countless denominations out there. Aside from the never-ending desire of publishers to make a profit, one of the main culprits behind this diversity is (you guessed it) the potential ambiguity of words.

The bulk of the Old Testament was of course written in ancient Hebrew, with a few instances of a related language called Aramaic. All the books of the New Testament were written in Greek. As you may know from an experience with Spanish, French, or some other language, there is never just one way to translate from one language to another. Different languages express themselves in different ways, and the range of meanings a word or phrase can have in one language is almost never the same as its equivalents in another. In other words, it is perfectly understandable that so many different translations could come from the same original texts.

English translations basically fall somewhere on a line in between two ends of a spectrum. On the one end

> There is always more than one way to translate words from one language to another.

are those translations that try to stick fairly closely to the original wording and sentence structure of the original Greek and Hebrew. These are "formal" equivalent translations like the King James Version, the New American

Standard Bible, or the English Standard Version. On the other end are those that more try to find concepts in our culture that roughly match the concepts of the original ones. These are "dynamic" equivalent translations like the New Living Translation or The New Century Version.[1]

Readers of versions like the New Living Translation love how understandable and readable they are. They often can't understand why someone wouldn't want to read something in as clear English as possible. Those who prefer versions like the Revised Standard Version protest that the ease of understanding comes at a cost. There is more than one way to interpret most sentences, and dynamic translations don't let the reader make any of the choices for him or herself. If the translation made the right choice, you'll see the meaning more clearly than ever. If it made an incorrect decision, you'll see a meaning clearly all right, but one that is incorrect.

For example, the New International Version (NIV) is somewhere in the middle of our spectrum. It is more formal than some and more dynamic than others. The Revised Standard Version, a formal equivalence translation, renders 1 Corinthians 7:1 as "It is well for a man not to touch a woman." The NIV, trying to make the verse clearer, translated it as "It is good for a man not to marry." If the NIV was correct, it made the verse much clearer.

But the NIV was almost certainly incorrect in this instance. Accordingly, the update of the NIV, Today's NIV, has corrected the translation: "It is good for a man not to have sexual relations with a woman." This time the translation has truly made the meaning clearer. We could mention any number of other controversial translations, particularly among versions aiming at more dynamic equivalents.

In one sense, dynamic equivalent translations are misleading. They are great for the clarity they have and the way they communicate. But they can mislead us into thinking the Bible was actually written in our categories and idiom. But of course the Bible was written in the categories of its ancient audiences, not in ours. At least one reason why formal equivalent translations are harder to read is because they actually reproduce the categories of the original meaning more accurately.

> No translation can do complete justice to the original meaning because our culture doesn't come equipped with all the same categories as those of the Bible's original cultures.

But ultimately no translation can do complete justice to the original meaning because our culture just doesn't come equipped with the same categories as those of the original cultures of the Bible. For example, we know that a sacrifice is when someone kills an animal and offers it to a god. But try as hard as I might, I don't think I'll ever really understand how the ancient psyche thought and experienced them.

The idea that I would kill an animal to appease the wrath of a god just isn't a concept that really translates easily to the Western world today. I can read words like "propitiation" and "expiation" in a translation (e.g., Romans 3:25, KJV, RSV)—even "sacrifice of atonement" (NIV, NRSV). But it's going to take a lot of work to "translate" the real dynamics of the Greek word behind these translations (*hilasterion*) into my categories.

More often than not we are unaware of how differently the words strike us than the way they struck their original audiences. Not that it is automatically bad for us to read the words differently, but part of our pilgrimage to a deeper understanding of Scripture is to realize how differently we read these words from the way they heard them. Here is a simple illustration. Matthew 5:45 says that God "causes it to rain on the righteous and the unrighteous." For a very long time I took this verse to mean that God allows bad things to happen to everyone from time to time—even to good people. It never even occurred to me to examine my own assumptions about rain. I grew up with the attitude, "Rain, rain, go away; please come back another today." So I unthinkingly assumed that the rain God was sending was bad.

Of course rain is a very good thing in an agrarian society where draught is all too common. In other words, the saying actually meant that God gives *good* things to everyone—even to bad people. Suddenly I noticed the context of the statement. It is in a paragraph where Jesus is saying to love our enemies. Matthew is using the example of God in this verse: if God can give good things even to those who are unrighteous, then I can love my enemies too.

We bring basic assumptions like these to every page of the Bible without even realizing it. The meanings that result for us are not necessarily wrong or contrary to God's purposes, but they are nonetheless different from the original meanings and connotations. For example, we miss a crucial element of the Parable of the Prodigal Son (Luke 15:11-32) if we think that feeding pigs in the story is only bad because pigs are so dirty (15:15-16). Since Jews were forbidden to eat pork or herd pigs (cf. Leviticus 11:7-8), we can infer that the wicked son of this story had not only left his father and village, he had left Israel and its faith as well.

Another element of the story we tend to miss in our culture are the honor/shame connotations the story

> We bring cultural assumptions to every page of the Bible, often without realizing it.

originally had. We miss how serious and shameful it was for a son to dishonor his father like these sons do in the story. These were acts many no doubt thought worthy of death (cf. Deuteronomy 21:21). We especially miss this aspect of the elder brother's actions, since we tend to sympathize with him. We miss the shame of an older man running, particularly to a dishonored son (15:20). Instead we process the story within our own categories.

I heard a story once of a missionary to Papua New Guinea who was struggling with how to convey the concept of Jesus as the lamb of God to a people who had little acquaintance with sheep. The missionary observed that pigs functioned in a similar way in their culture. So he translated the concept for them as "Jesus is the pig of God."

To our ears this sounds disrespectful, because a pig is dirty to us and undesirable in our cultural dictionary. It is so difficult for us to realize that so many of the things that seem self-evident and obvious to us are simply assumptions and constructs we inherited from our culture as a child. We subtly change the connotations of the Bible's words all the time without even realizing it.

In the end, the meaning of "pig" for us is not the absolute meaning of a pig. After all, the Gospel of Mark declares all foods clean (Mark 7:19). And we no doubt don't even realize how differently *we* probably understand the phrase "lamb of God" from the Bible's original audiences. The connotations we see in these words are more often than not constructs of our culture, just as they are for Bible readers from other cultures as well. In this case, "pig of God" proved to convey the meaning of the Bible for the New Guineans far better than "lamb of God" did.

Filling in "Gaps" in the Story

Some of the most helpful sermons and Christian books today are those that subtly "fill in the gaps" of the biblical story with contemporary cultural assumptions. What was Mary feeling when she became pregnant, knowing what everyone was thinking about her? What was going through Noah's head as he obeyed God and started building an ark—when he had never seen rain before?

Max Lucado is an extremely popular Christian author. We can tell how great his ministry to Christians is today by how well his books sell. We will find him and other Christian authors and preachers filling in the gaps of the biblical story in exactly these sorts of ways. It is often at these points that we find them most ministering to our felt needs.[2]

For example, Lucado's book *And the Angels Were Silent* takes us through the final week of Jesus' earthly life.[3] Throughout, Lucado addresses the kinds of questions we might have about the motives of various individuals and what they were thinking and feeling. Why did the disciples keep the blind men away from Jesus? What did it mean to Jesus for Simon to invite him over to his house? How did Simon feel toward Jesus after Jesus healed him of leprosy? These are the kinds of questions that naturally jump into our minds as we read the biblical text.

We regularly fill in gaps like these as we read the Bible. These are often the parts of the sermon we enjoy the most and find most relevant. After all, it is often the significance of the questions for our lives that leads us to ask them of the text. And the answers we see are usually those that seem to make the most sense in our lives.

> The questions we bring to the Biblical text determine the answers we find there, and these usually have more to do with our context than with those of the original audiences.

As you might expect, the questions we raise of the Biblical text usually have more to do with our context than with that of the Bible's original audiences. After all, we naturally ask about the kinds of things that flow directly from our lives. Yet our lives and world are different from the lives and worlds of the original audiences of the Bible. In other words, the questions they asked of these texts were likely much different from ours. Since the questions you ask largely determine the meanings you take from the text, we see once again how the meaning of these same words subtly shifts from person to person and from culture to culture. The answers we give to our questions will frequently differ significantly from anything the original authors and audiences had in mind.

What five leadership principles can we take from Paul's writings? What three lessons on failure can I learn from Peter? What can I learn from Job about surviving suffering? In each case the question is something very pertinent to my life today. But we are bound to approach these issues with unconscious cultural assumptions about leadership, guilt, and feelings, reading into these ancient individuals the categories of a modern, Western individualist.

Again, I ultimately believe God speaks to us in this way. But we should note on our pilgrimage just how differently people of other cultures, times, and places have thought and experienced the world. Indeed, an African is far more likely to read these texts with the "right" cultural assumptions than someone from the Western world.

We alluded earlier in the chapter to the fact that the ancient world largely operated with the categories of honor and shame. The Western world is much more of an individualist "guilt culture." In other words, the Western world formulates personal identity largely in terms of individuals. In contrast, most people throughout history—including those in the Bible—belonged to "group" cultures where their identity had everything to do with the groups to which they belonged.

We can catch a glimpse of the difference by looking at marriage customs. Because we define ourselves so extensively as individuals in our culture, we practice "dating" in preparation for marriage to see if we are "compatible" with one another. Do you squeeze your toothpaste in the middle or roll it from the end? Do you drink coffee? Regular or decaf? With cream, milk, or black—half and half okay? Cappuccino? Mocha Java? Burger King used to have a jingle: "Hold the pickle, hold the lettuce; special orders don't upset us."

People from other cultures find this degree of "individuation" in Western, particularly American culture, astounding. Accordingly, we tend to be introspective and self-preoccupied. We want to be known "for who we are," not because of our relationships to other people. We live for ourselves rather than for our families, our nation, or the other groups to which we belong. And when we do marry, we want to have intimate relationships where our innermost needs and desires are fulfilled.

Other cultures, including much of the Bible world, have marriages arranged—sometimes even before the children are born. Basically, two people are compatible if they come from the right genders, families, and races. Divorce is less common in group cultures in part because marriage is not viewed as an intimate relationship between two people. Identity is much more an external feature of a person than an internal one.

Women are one way, men another. There are exceptions, but they usually involve shame. Greeks are this way; Jews are that way. Conformity to our common values is honorable; the independent thinker is a deviant. There are group-sanctioned ambitions, but the roles are well defined by the culture. Individuals are stereotyped into certain fixed categories—people don't change their character; they stay the same from birth. Acceptance of your lot in life is more the name of the game than personal responsibility for "what you do with your life."

In contrast, we are introspective and intimate in orientation. We want deep fellowship where we share our innermost, personal secrets. We value a "personal relationship with Jesus Christ." These are largely foreign categories to the biblical world, as to much of the world outside the West today. I see myself as an individual when I read the word *you* in the Bible, as if it is addressed to me individually. In reality, "you" is more often than not plural in the Bible and addressed to whole communities of faith.

Not too long ago another very popular Christian book came out called the *Prayer of Jabez*.[4] Again, this book must have ministered greatly to Christians simply on the basis of how many copies sold. This small book found incredible significance in a one verse prayer by an otherwise unknown person named Jabez, hidden in the middle of a seemingly endless family tree (1 Chronicles 3:10). In the book, Bruce Wilkinson does what we all tend to do when we read the Bible: he puts himself into Jabez's "shoes" and looks around.

Of course much of what Wilkinson finds thus relates significantly to the way we think as individualists. Jabez looks back on past struggles with nervousness. He feels vulnerable and has a sense of urgency. He steps out in faith and asks God to enlarge his borders. We relate to this Jabez, because this is the way we would feel if we were in his situation. Accordingly, his story ministers to us.

But the historical Jabez would not likely recognize much in this book. Here is a man who successfully fought against the people who lived around him and expanded the territory of his family. To do so he no doubt killed some of them and perhaps left others without their homes. These accomplishments gained him honor among his people, for the acquisition of land was a value of his culture.

We are not told that he was attacked or that his neighbors were hostile. The Bible does not tell us that his motives were to purify the land. There was no command from God to obliterate the Canaanites. It is far more likely culturally that Jabez was simply ambitious, and God granted him success.

My point is not to deny that God prospered Jabez. Indeed, we troublingly find any number of other places in the Old Testament where God seems to sanction the killing and plundering of other peoples, including the slaughter of women and children (e.g., Josh. 6:21). But the thought processes of individuals like Joshua and Jabez did not work anything like the way ours work as individualist Christians today.

Because we bring our cultural dictionary to the words of the Bible, its words and stories often take on a kind of "mirror" quality in which we see ourselves and our lives. As we do with movies and stories today, we will often find that we identify with one of the characters in the biblical story. That character in the divine story becomes a catalyst through which we see ourselves, both our strengths and our weaknesses. We fill in the gaps of the story with filler that makes sense given our cultural and theological assumptions. We connect the pieces with the glue of our perspectives on life and the world.

> We fill in the gaps of the story with filler that makes sense given our cultural and theological assumptions. We connect the pieces with the glue of our perspectives on life and the world. The words and stories take on a mirror quality in which, by the Spirit, we see ourselves and our lives.

The words of the Bible in this respect are therapeutic for us, sacramental. The Holy Spirit leads us to self-knowledge by way of the text. The truths we see are indeed truths about ourselves, even if they often have little or nothing to do with the meaning the texts originally had. I see nothing wrong with this process, especially if we engage in it with a clear awareness of how God is speaking as we read.

Spiritual Common Sense

There are some instances where it is fairly easy to spot cultural aspects of the biblical text. My Christian "brother" might not react too well if I went up to him and greeted him "with a holy kiss" (1 Thessalonians 5:26). And from the look of things most Christian women don't feel that they need to cover their heads when they pray in church—or even that it is wrong for them to have short hair for that matter (1 Corinthians 11:5-6). Christians have goatees (Leviticus 19:27), eat pork (11:7), and wear polyester (Leviticus 19:19; Deuteronomy 22:11) regularly without a thought.

Christians who pass over passages like these implicitly acknowledge that the books of the Bible were originally written to contexts that were different from ours. They are using what I like to call "spiritual common sense." These are instances where we might not fully be able to explain why we don't feel compelled to follow the letter of the Bible. But most Christians have nevertheless come to the same basic conclusion. They have "caught the Spirit" on the issue in question.

Christian men who don't greet each other in church with a kiss and Christian women who don't veil their heads in prayer implicitly acknowledge that some of the biblical material was written to address a different culture.

Of course there are a number of Christian groups that do try to take every word of the Bible as if it addressed them directly. Mennonite women wear prayer bonnets on their heads. And there are a number of Christian groups in which the men do greet each other from time to time with a kiss on the cheek. I even know of Christians who try to keep the food laws of Leviticus regarding pork and other animals forbidden in Leviticus.

I deeply respect Christians who demonstrate such a high degree of devotion, especially in a broader culture that views them as oddities and the butt of jokes. At the same time, this approach to Scripture is subject to any number of critiques. One is of course the fact that doing what the ancients did is not "doing what they did" in the sense that the meaning is not the same. There were reasons for God's commands; they were not rules given simply for their own sake. A woman who uncovers her head in worship today is not shaming her husband, as the women of Corinth possibly were (1 Corinthians 11:5). The act has no significance for us today; it has become an insignificant act.

More importantly, the Bible itself as a whole does not model an unchanging ethic or teaching.

> Doing what the ancients did is not doing what they did if the significance of the action is different.

Seventh-Day Adventists do not worship on Sundays, in contrast to the vast majority of Christians. Nevertheless, they have rightly recognized that the Jewish Sabbath of Exodus 20:8 took place from sundown on Friday to sundown on Saturday. Accordingly, they worship on Saturdays.

> The Bible itself as a whole does not model an unchanging ethic.

However, in so doing they ignore two things. The first is that all the evidence we have from the New Testament indicates that the early Christians worshipped on Sundays.[5] They came together on the first day of the week, Sunday (Acts 20:7; 1 Corinthians 16:2). The witness of the early Christians from the early 100's makes it clear that this was the tradition of the earliest Christians—to get together on Sunday in memory of Christ's resurrection (Mark 16:2).

Secondly, the New Testament does not consider Sabbath observance binding for Christians, particularly non-Jewish Christians—even though it was one of the Ten Commandments! Colossians 2:16 says, "do not let someone judge you in food and in drink or in the matter of a festival, a new moon, or sabbaths." Paul similarly says in Romans 14:5: "One person considers one day more significant than another, another person considers every day alike. Let each be fully convinced in his [or her] own mind." In other words, it is up to the conscience of the individual Christian as to whether s/he observes the Jewish Sabbath.

Some who look for a unified meaning in the Bible have tried to harmonize these statements with the Old Testament in one way or another. For example, many Christians "glue" the pieces together by supposing that Sunday has taken the place of the Jewish Sabbath. Some even transfer the commandment not to work on the Sabbath (Exodus 20:9) to Sunday. Thus in the movie *Chariots of Fire*, a Scottish runner refuses to run in the Olympics on Sunday as a matter of conscience.

But the New Testament never equates Sunday with the Jewish Sabbath, and the New Testament actually forbids requiring a Christian to observe the Jewish Sabbath. Someone might object, "But the Sabbath was instituted at creation" (Genesis 2:2; Exodus 20:11). I know—isn't it amazing that God would allow such a drastic change in what he expects of his people?

The main difference between Jesus and the Pharisees in the gospels and between Paul and his opponents at Galatia is that both Jesus and Paul used "spiritual common sense" when they applied the Bible's words. They followed the "spirit" rather than the letter of the Scripture (2 Corinthians 3:6). While the Pharisees were concerned about the Sabbath law, Jesus was concerned with his disciples getting fed (Mark 2:23-28). While James was concerned with the purity laws of Leviticus, Paul was concerned with the unity of Jewish and non-Jewish believers (Galatians 2:11).

Jesus summed up the rule of thumb well when he said "The sabbath came into existence for people, not people for the sabbath" (Mark 2:27). In other words, a person's life is more important than a rule, even if it is one of the Ten Commandments. Jesus backed up these ideas with an astounding reminder of an incident that took place in the days of King David (Mark 2:25-26). David's soldiers were hungry, and a priest allowed them to eat bread from the sanctuary (1 Samuel 21:1-6). This priest was way out of line according to the law (Leviticus 24:9). But he was right on target with regard to the Spirit.

Many see an opportunity for abuse in anything but an absolutist ethic that does not allow for exceptions. On the one hand, they are right—we are prone

> Except for the command to love, neither Jesus nor Paul were legalistic or absolutist in their appropriation of Scripture.

to "take a mile" when given an inch. And we as humans cannot always be sure when people are sincere and when they are taking advantage of a "loophole" in the rules. Further, our "common sense" can mislead us—the "common sense" of one person isn't always the sense of someone else.

And can't cultures be wrong? Isn't part of the Bible's role to be counter-cultural? What if we find that American culture as a whole comes to accept homosexuality? Does that mean that God approves of homosexuality and that Paul was only thinking "culturally" when he wrote?

These are all the right kinds of questions and concerns. Allowing for the cultural dimension of the Bible makes applying the Bible to today a "messier" and more imprecise process than we prefer. Allowing for changes in the rules over time and for exceptional circumstances does not give us the clarity of a "God said it; I believe it; that settles it for me."

But we must press on for several reasons. The first is that we are simply stuck with this situation. As the ancient saying goes, "Abuse is no excuse." I cannot deny a truth or the correct action simply because someone might abuse it. The Bible was written in the categories of the ancients. The New Testament does modify the teaching and requirements of the Old Testament. And the New Testament teaching will not play itself out the same way today unless we translate it into our categories. It would be easier if I could just apply the words directly to myself, but this tactic almost always leads to the path of the Pharisees Jesus opposed and the "literalists" Paul opposed.

We are also getting our own role out of perspective. God is ultimately the judge and the one who dispenses judgment (Hebrews 10:30). Certainly the Bible also models confronting those who have spiritual problems (Matthew 19:15; 1 Corinthians 5:5). But ultimately "catching the wrong-doer" is God's business, not ours. Someone might escape our notice, someone might "get away" with something down here. But God sees, and God knows (Romans 14:22; Hebrews 4:13).

Most importantly of all is the fact that it is the nature of love to be willing to bend and make exceptions. When my son was two years old, he was very talented at opening things. We put a special knob on the front door, but it seems like he was the only one in the house who could actually turn it. We put special gizmos on certain windows, but he could still open them.

Let's say I had told our baby sitter during that time not to let Tommy out of the house. "I'm afraid he'll run out into the street," I might have said. Let's even say I became emphatic: "Under no circumstances are you to let Tommy out of the house."

Then let's say our house caught on fire. Can you imagine the baby-sitter telling Tommy, "I'm sorry, Tommy. I know you're going to burn, but your Dad said I wasn't to let you out of the house"? Of course not! The right course of action would be immediately obvious—take exception to my rule and get him out!

Christians regularly take the Bible's words in rigid ways that are like this legalistic baby-sitter. In so doing they read the words significantly out of proportion to the limits originally intended. What if a husband beat his wife regularly, but never had an affair? Let's say he claimed to be a Christian and didn't want a divorce. Let's say he commanded his wife to stay with him and forbade her to leave the house.

You could make a case from the Bible's words that she must stay with him. He hasn't had an affair, so she cannot divorce him (Matthew 5:32). He is pleased to live with her, even if we conclude he is not really a Christian—thus she is still bound to him (1 Corinthians 7:13). Further, 1 Peter 3:1-6 describes a situation in which a wife accepts the authority of her husband even if he is an unbeliever: "Sarah obeyed Abraham and called him lord" (3:6).

God forbid! It would go soundly against the Spirit of Christ for us to tell a woman in this situation that she must remain with this man. God no doubt shakes his head at Christians who read the Bible so out of focus with his Spirit. Jesus would no doubt look at us with complete disbelief if we presented this way of using his words back to him. It goes against every example he has left us. "I never intended those words to be used in a situation like that," he would say to us. We have twisted words intended to benefit God's people and made them instruments of torture.

> To be faithful to God's Spirit, we must be flexible in the way we appropriate Scripture, allowing both for exceptional circumstances and changing cultures.

To be faithful to God's Spirit, there must be flexibility in the way we appropriate Scripture that allows both for exceptional circumstances and changing cultures. We will also want some sort of "check" to make sure we also allow for God to critique our culture. With individuals, the best check is for us to read the Bible together. By reading in community we subject ourselves to the critique of other Christians with the Spirit inside them.

We can balance and check the short-sightedness of our culture by reading the Bible in community with Christians of other cultures. Even better yet, we should become aware of how other Christians throughout the ages have read these words. If the Spirit lives in the entire body of Christ, then the more other Christians we read with, the more likely we are to "catch the Spirit."

Guiding Principle One: Loving Interpretation

The guiding principle behind "spiritual common sense" is love. When Jesus was asked what the greatest commandment was, he responded "'You will love the Lord your God with all your heart and with all your soul and with all your mind.' This is the greatest and first commandment. And the second is like it: 'You will love your neighbor as yourself.' On these two commandments all the Law and the prophets hang" (Matthew 22:37-40).

Other New Testament writers, particularly Paul (Romans 13:8-10; Galatians 5:14) and James (James 2:8), say exactly the same thing. Notice that Jesus taught that we must love our enemies (Matthew 5:43-48). He certainly believed we should love our friends. No one is left—God requires us to love everyone.

What this observation means is that any appropriation of the Bible that involves hatred of someone is incorrect; it is not a Christian use of Scripture. Some forms of Christianity get so focused on the words of the Bible that they forget Christ's bottom line. They bring the Bible's words into contradiction with Christ. Clearly Christ trumps any biblical interpretation that involves hatred of a human being—it would be wrong to obey the "Bible" of this person.

We have arrived at the first of two basic "guidelines" for the Christian use of the Bible's words. I would argue that any interpretation that fits

> Any appropriation of the Bible that is in keeping with love of our neighbor is appropriate; any appropriation that involves hatred of a person is not Christian.

with these two guidelines is an appropriate interpretation of Scripture, even if it has nothing to do with the original meaning. The first guideline concerns interpretations that relate to how we should live. Here the guiding principle is love. Any appropriation of Scripture that is in keeping with love of our neighbor is appropriate; any appropriation that involves hatred of a person is not Christian.[6]

We saw in chapter one that the Bible has any number of verses that a person could use to justify an evil action: "Blessed are those who take and dash your little ones against the rock!" (Psalms 137:9). We saw in the previous chapter that Jesus filtered Old Testament teaching through the lens of love. He holds the magnet of love up to the Old Testament law. Whatever sticks he retains; whatever doesn't falls by the way.

Thus in some instances the requirement is deepened: it is wrong to even contemplate adultery, not just to do it (Matthew 5:27-28). In other cases the law becomes obsolete because the principle of love undermines the very reason the law existed in the first place. Thus the person who is truthful does not need to make oaths at all because his or her word stands on its own as trustworthy (Matt. 5:33-37). In still other cases it becomes wrong to keep the law, such as when the law of retaliation says to "show no pity" in the exacting of retribution (Deut. 19:21; Matt. 5:38-42).

While it may stretch our way of thinking, the same must also apply to the way we use the New Testament today. There may be teaching in the New Testament that would not play itself out in the spirit of love today if we enacted it rigidly. New Testament teaching on issues like whether we should eat with a disobedient Christian (e.g., 1 Corinthians 5:9-11; 2 Thessalonians 3:14) may or may not accomplish Paul's goals in our context. We could argue that the church has already abolished slavery as a fundamentally unchristian practice, even though the New Testament implicitly accepts it (e.g., Colossians 3:12-4:1).

Of course deciding what is loving and what is not needs to be a corporate rather than an individual task. While we must ultimately decide how to live as individual Christians, deciding such things in communities of faith helps us "catch the Spirit" more accurately than as individuals. This process is bound to involve some frustration, especially for those of us who want hard and fast, black and white answers. But this process is part of what it is to "work out your own salvation with fear and trembling" (Philippians 2:12). The word *you* is plural here, and Paul refers to that corporate process of helping each other make it to the end. So too we must struggle to figure out the specifics of what God requires of us in every generation, time, and place.

---

[1] Versions like the New International Version and Today's New International Version stand somewhere in the middle.

[2] D. Drury and J. Drury have written an article entitled, "'Purpose Driven Catechism': Is *The Purpose Driven Life* the Evangelical Catechism." In this article they argue that R. Warren's best selling book gives us a snapshot of the faith values of current evangelical culture.

[3] *And the Angels Were Silent: The Final Week of Jesus* (Portland: Multnomah, 1992).

[4] Bruce Wilkinson, *The Prayer of Jabez: Breaking Through to the Blessed Life* (Portland: Multnomah, 2000).

[5] Actually, the evidence seems to indicate that Jewish Christians did continue to observe the Jewish Sabbath (e.g., Acts 17:2) in addition to the "Lord's Day" on Sunday (cf. Revelation 1:10).

[6] Of course the Bible also portrays God as a God of justice and holiness. But these other dimensions of God's revealed character do not contradict the absoluteness of Jesus' love ethic *for us*. For one thing, I am not God. The New Testament rarely envisages the Christian individual or community as agents of God's justice.

Secondly, justice in its purest sense is blind. In this sense neither hatred nor love determine what would be just, and justice can be administered without hate or prejudice. Finally, the teaching of Jesus implies that mercy ultimately triumphs over justice and judgment in terms of how we are to live our lives on earth (Matthew 18:21-35; 23:23; James 2:13). In other words, mercy is a higher principle than justice for the Christian in this world.

Chapter 4
When Scholars Decide

A Seminarian's Tale

Seminaries are graduate schools where most of the students are preparing to become ministers. In many denominations you can't be fully ordained unless you have a seminary degree called a Masters of Divinity. Seminaries are professional schools—they don't necessarily presume that you have studied religion previously. The result is that you will often find a number of second career students at a seminary whose first careers had nothing to do with religion at all.

We can tell a tale that many, though not all seminarians have experienced. Many have entered their study of the Bible at a university or seminary with great enthusiasm and vigor. Perhaps the person has heard God calling them to ministry and is eager to "save the lost," to spread the good news. Maybe they have even risked a change in career in the excitement of serving God's people. This individual may be someone who hears God's voice regularly in the words of the Bible and is thrilled with daily reading from the "Word." They are excited to think of getting a degree that involves serious study of the Bible.

They then experience something like the pilgrimage of this book. They learn how to read the words of the Bible in context. Resist though they might, the facts are irresistible. They increasingly realize that these words were not originally addressed to them. They once heard God's voice leap off the pages of the Bible without any thought of the original context. Now they get bogged down in things like Greek and "word studies." They take professor after professor and find not only that each one is absolutely convinced he or she has the correct interpretation. They also find that these teachers frequently disagree with each other on what that "correct" interpretation actually is.

A recent conservative book on the process of biblical interpretation helps make our point.[1] It outlines a four step process for appropriating the Bible for today: 1) determine the original application, 2) evaluate the level of specificity of the original application, 3) identify cross-cultural principles, and 4) find appropriate applications that embody the broader principles.[2]

This procedure makes perfect sense in the light of our pilgrimage thus far. First you figure out what the Bible meant originally in its original context. Then you determine how closely that teaching was connected with the specific context it was addressing. You separate the "all time" significance of this teaching from that which related specifically to "that time" and "that instance." With these principles in hand, you reapply the teaching to "our time."

The mind of the seminarian has now become incredibly enlightened with this dose of seminary medicine. But there are also several potential side-effects. Many have lost the joy of reading the Bible they once had. It is now hard work that involves commentaries, dictionaries, and grammar books. Of course some are thrilled at the challenge and find the process exhilarating. Others subconsciously feel empowered with a secret knowledge of Greek and Hebrew that they can use to trump the uninitiated.

Some now feel incompetent to interpret the Bible. They see no way they will ever be able to interpret with the incredible genius and skills they have seen in their professors. They have either consciously or unconsciously decided not to preach from the Bible in their ministries. Perhaps their grades have told them they have no business talking about what the Bible means. Even if they were once confident about what God has to say, they now feel thoroughly indecisive about what the Bible really means.

For others the meaning of the Bible has become irrelevant. They have understood what it means to read in context, and they now see little connection between its world and their world. They've also decided consciously or unconsciously not to use Scripture in their preaching. Perhaps they have even become angry at the Bible and at those who speak of its authority and inspiration.

> If we have to know the original meaning to hear God's voice in Scripture, then the vast majority of Christians who have lived for the last two thousand years are in trouble.

We get the sneaking suspicion that if the Bible is truly "God's Word," it must somehow work more simply than this complicated process. What of the illiterate medieval peasant whose best knowledge of the Bible came from the pictures on the stained glass windows on the nearby cathedral? After all, the mass and Scripture were read in Latin. What of the countless Christians out there who really do seem to hear God's voice in the words of Scripture—even though the meaning they see has little or nothing to do with what it meant originally? In short, if we have to know the original meaning to hear God's voice in Scripture, then the vast majority of Christians who have lived for the last two thousand years are in trouble.

The Uncertainty of the Original Meaning

We can raise a number of other questions about the quest for the Bible's original meaning. We have already raised the question of relevance. Even more difficult is the question of whether we can even know the original meaning with certainty. Suppose that you have studied enough to be counted among those who know the most about the Bible. You have become an expert at Greek, Hebrew, and Aramaic grammar and have an exhaustive knowledge of ancient history and literature. You know a great deal about what words could mean in the ancient world, as well as its varied cultural and historical settings.

Suppose you have also become a master of the voluminous history of interpretation for every passage in the Bible. You have read every book, every article, and know all the possible interpretations that have been made throughout history. Even if we could find scholars of this caliber, they would doubtlessly still disagree on the original meaning of countless passages in the

Bible. We simply do not have enough information on the original contexts of these individual writings to conclude definitively on countless different issues.

One of the more puzzling passages in the New Testament to me is found in 2 Thessalonians 2. This passage addresses the question of how the Thessalonians will know when the

> We simply do not have enough information on the original contexts of these individual writings to conclude definitively on countless different issues.

"Day of the Lord," Judgment Day, has arrived. Of course the first thing that strikes me is how they could even have this question. I have grown up with such a cataclysmic sense of God's judgment that I can hardly fathom how someone could think it had already happened. Here is the first hint that my assumptions must be significantly different in some way from those of the Thessalonians.

The letter talks somewhat cryptically about the things that will happen in the time leading up to the Day of the Lord. It speaks of a "rebellion" and a "man of lawlessness" who "takes his seat in the temple of God" (2 Thessalonians 2:3-4). But it does not say who is rebelling or what temple. The temple of Paul's day was destroyed in AD70, and the passage says nothing about a temple being rebuilt in the future, let alone about the one that was standing then being destroyed.

The passage goes on: "Do you not remember that I told you these things when I was still with you?" (2 Thessalonians 2:5). Here is a painful demonstration that this letter was not written to me. I don't remember Paul talking about these things because I was not there in Thessalonica. This letter was not addressed to me. I don't know what rebellion or man of lawlessness he told them about.

The ambiguity gets worse: "[Y]ou know *what* is restraining him" (2 Thessalonians 2:6). Yes, the Thessalonians knew, but I don't. The passage then shifts from talking about *what* is holding the man of lawlessness back to *who* is holding him back: "until *the one who* now restrains it is removed. And then the lawless one will be revealed" (2:7-8). I can make some educated guesses about what this letter was talking about, but we ultimately don't have enough information to decide with certainty. Gaps like these in our background knowledge put a huge damper on any effort to know the original meaning of the Bible—and thus on any claim that the authoritative meaning of the Bible is the original meaning.

Paul's view of the Jewish law provides us with an excellent case in point. A group of diverse, internationally renowned scholars of Paul's writings gathered together in 1995 in the hope of reaching some consensus on Paul's attitude toward the law of Moses.[3] After a week of discussion, some of the most distinguished Pauline scholars of an entire generation were unable to reach consensus on the issue.

Time and time again we will find that scholars disagree wildly on the meaning and/or significance of a passage. It is not that we can't identify more and less likely interpretations. Indeed, we can eliminate a great deal of interpretations fairly easily. Thus anyone who would argue that the gospels originally viewed Jesus as the "bad guy" is clearly mistaken.

But even within the clear bounds of context we can almost always find room for multiple potentially valid interpretations. Even when we have tried our best to take off our personal, denominational, and cultural glasses, we will find ambiguity. Even if we resist the urge to harmonize and make the meaning fit with what we already believe, uncertainty will still abound. The original meaning may be a more stable meaning than the passing trends of individuals, churches, and cultures. But it is still potentially quite uncertain.

Changing Scholarly Paradigms

The previous chapter mentioned how church groups often have very specific perspectives they bring to the biblical text, "rules" for how to process the things the Bible says. We compared these "glasses" or frameworks of thought to scientific paradigms and theories. I talked about how a church might have a very specific understanding of the Spirit that it brings to every place where the Bible mentions the Spirit.

We observe in the history of the Bible's interpretation that the scholarly guild of interpreters also runs through various phases in which a particular paradigm is in vogue. Then we will see a revolution in perspective, leading to a new paradigm. There is always the possibility that some new treasure trove of ancient manuscripts will be found that completely revolutionizes the perspectives about which scholars are now so convinced. This ongoing possibility of a future paradigm shift also calls into question the all-sufficiency of the original meaning of the Bible as an absolute path to God's voice.

> We face the ongoing possibility that some new evidence or hypothesis will completely revolutionize the perspectives about which scholars are currently so convinced.

On the one hand, I am not completely pessimistic about these changing revolutions. We can identify a number of ideas that have basically remained the same since scholars began to read the Bible's original meaning with a heightened awareness of its ancient context. We can thus identify certain constants throughout the last two centuries. Further, while new evidence could certainly alter our understanding of countless things, we do have an adequate sampling of material from the ancient world to make reasonable suggestions about the big picture of that world.

And the amount of scholarly attention to the minute possibilities of the biblical text is astounding. For example, there were already at least forty different interpretations of 1 Corinthians 15:29 by 1950.[4] With so many budding scholars scouring over the text, all looking to make their mark by way of some new, groundbreaking interpretation, surely most of the possible ways of reading a verse like this one have already been suggested by someone somewhere.

We all know that a multiple choice test is easier than a "fill in the blank" one. In other words, the scholarship of today is more likely to be aware of the "naughty data" that creates paradigm shifts than the scholars of even fifty years ago. It's easier to be a good scholar today because you have so many different shoulders to stand on and so many electronic research tools and databases at your disposal. So even if we can identify 30 different possible interpretations of 1 Corinthians 6:18, there are only two really strong candidates.[5]

One example of a scholarly perspective that has remained constant for over a hundred years deals with the relationship between Matthew, Mark, and Luke. The wording of Matthew, Mark, and Luke is so similar at times that some literary relationship almost certainly existed between them. In other words, either they have used each other as sources in some way or they come from a common source. The similarity in wording is not simply a matter of Jesus' words, so it is not just that the disciples remembered what Jesus had said.[6] The verbal similarity extends to how the story is told, even to how it is summarized (e.g., Matthew 8:16; Mark 1:32-34; Luke 4:40). And the same basic stories are also laid out in the same basic order, the same basic collection in a life that included countless more events than these.

Since the late 1800's the explanation that most scholars have given for this phenomenon is that Mark was written first and that Matthew and Luke then used Mark to provide a basic framework for their own gospels. They then supplemented Mark with their own sources, perhaps even one other major source that they both shared in common. We could list countless other proposals that scholars have made over the last century and a half, but none have ever supplanted the "prevailing paradigm," which we might call "Markan priority."

But this is not to say that we have not witnessed some significant "paradigm changes" as well. In particular, the last two decades have seen an explosion in the study of oral tradition and the gospels, the recognition that the ancient world was far more oriented around speaking and hearing than around writing and reading. This development has brought with it a greater recognition of how the process of story-telling works in an oral culture. We remember that the stereotypical poet who told the stories of Homer was blind and recited forty-eight chapters worth of story from memory. Today we recognize illiterate Muslims who can quote the entire Quran from memory.

These considerations have caused gospel scholars to modify their paradigms somewhat. It is not as unfeasible as it used to be that oral tradition of gospel length could be memorized and passed along orally. Perhaps even more significantly, we cannot dismiss the historicity of Jesus' words and of events in the gospels simply because they may have gone through a phase in which they were passed along by word of mouth and not written down. In other words, oral tradition may vary wording and details around the edges, but in general it is a reliable way of passing information.[7]

To be sure, these considerations have affected the century old consensus on how the gospels came together. The new "oral paradigm" has brought an interesting re-examination of Markan priority. But Markan priority remains the prevailing hypothesis. In other words, even though scholars have modified their paradigm somewhat and we find a less certain guild than twenty years ago, this theory has stood the test of time. It remains the hypothesis most scholars think best fits the evidence we have.[8] It is an example of a scholarly consensus that has remained constant over time despite amazing developments that have taken place around it.

I also believe that changes in paradigm like these can move us closer to understanding the original meaning. For example, the recent consideration of orality has actually moved us closer to understanding the original meaning and history of the words in the gospels. We can identify a similar revolution in the understanding of Paul that has taken place in the last thirty years among Pauline scholars, sometimes called the "new perspective" on Paul.

Up until the 1970's, scholarship interpreted Paul through the eyes of what I might call a "Lutheran paradigm." To put it in oversimplified terms, Paul was an individual racked with guilt at his inability to keep the law, to keep from sinning. Judaism was a religion in which you had to be good for God to accept you—you had to earn your salvation. But try and try though he might, Paul was beset with a constant sense of defeat.

In a moment of conversion, Paul realized that no one was good enough for God to accept him or her on the basis of how s/he lived. Paul discovered the doctrine of "justification by faith alone," the idea that God declares us "not guilty" of our sin on the basis of our belief in Christ rather than by our deeds or works. This doctrine became the centerpiece of Paul's ministry from then on, as the Jewish Saul became the Christian Paul.

In the last thirty years, scholarship has challenged almost every comment in the last two paragraphs. In many cases scholars have done so in a way that is thoroughly convincing. At some points this "new perspective" on Paul makes so much better sense of the evidence that we are amazed it took so long for us to see it.

For example, Paul's writings do not really give us the sense that he struggled with a guilty conscience.[9] Certainly Martin Luther did, the father of Protestantism and the lens through which the scholars of the last four hundred years read Paul. But Paul himself does not give off these signals. Words like "forgiveness" and "repentance" only appear sporadically in his writings, while Paul frequently tells his audiences to imitate him (e.g., 1 Cor. 11:1)—something that indicates confidence rather than a sense of inadequacy. Indeed, Paul says that he kept the Jewish law blamelessly before he came to Christ (Philippians 3:6). The key passage that earlier generations took as a "guilty Paul" (Romans 7:9-24) seems more a theoretical discussion than an autobiographical one.[10] In short, the pre-Christian Paul was probably much more like the Pharisee of Luke 18:9-14 than the young Martin Luther.

Further, the bulk of the Jewish literature at our disposal indicates that Judaism was as much a religion of grace as of works.[11] Jews would have agreed with Paul that "all have sinned" and would have agreed that we can only find acceptance with God because he is gracious. Luther at this point once again read his own debates against the Roman Catholic Church into Paul's debates with his opponents. Paul's debates focused more on whether a non-Jew needed to keep specific aspects of the *Jewish* law in order to be accepted by God, rather than whether we could earn our way to heaven by way of "good works." And for Jews, it was not a question of "getting in"; it was a matter of responding appropriately to God's grace—"staying in."[12]

Several other aspects to earlier paradigms about Paul have also faced challenge in these years. Was justification by faith really the central element in Paul's thought, since he only really draws on the concept extensively in Romans and Galatians? Did Paul really focus on faith *in* Christ or should the phrase be translated the "faithfulness *of* Christ"? Should we really think of Paul being "converted"—did he really think that he changed religions when he came to Christ? Certainly it is wrong to think that Paul changed his name from Saul to Paul when he came to Christ. Acts continues to call him Saul even ten years after he became a Christian.

Of course the new perspective on Paul has been around long enough for it to be challenged as a paradigm also.[13] And we probably cannot identify any consensus yet on the items in the preceding paragraph. But I believe we have seen definite breakthroughs in our understanding of Paul. I think we genuinely understand Paul better today than we did forty years ago. While the new paradigm may change in its details, I think it too will stand the test of time.

Yet the fact that biblical paradigms can change so drastically must give us pause. What if they unearth some new cache of ancient documents tomorrow? What if those new documents put an entirely different spin on issues we had long since thought settled? The Dead Sea Scrolls had this effect when they first appeared. Despite our confidence on various issues, we will never be sure we have it right while we are on earth.

We can identify any number of other paradigms that have come and gone, leaving us wonder how anyone ever believed them. A notorious one is the myth of the Gnostic Redeemer that pervaded the scholarship of the early twentieth century. According to this paradigm, a movement known as

Gnosticism pervaded the ancient world at the time of Christ. This Gnosticism taught about a heavenly being who came down to earth from the realm of light to rescue humans, who are sparks of light imprisoned in material bodies. According to this paradigm, the early Christians took Jesus to be this heavenly being and incorporated him into the myth.

But of course this paradigm has almost no legitimate basis for it whatsoever. We have no direct

> Despite current scholarly confidence on many issues, in the end we can never be certain that we have it right.

evidence that the Gnostic movement even existed in any coherent form until the second century after Christ. Some of the primary sources used to construct the theory date to the 600's and 700's—astoundingly later than the New Testament. The theory can only work if we piece it together from scattered comments here and there at the time of Christ and suppose *hypothetically* that they all existed together somewhere at the time, even though no instance of it has survived.

In the end, it is much more likely that the Christian message came first, and these later Gnostic texts drew *from it*. This suggestion fits the evidence we have much better. Hypotheses are like pictures we draw out of the data available to us, data that is like dots of evidence on a page. A good hypothesis is one that sticks closely to the available dots, incorporating most of them into its picture and not drawing too much where there are no dots. Like so many paradigms that shift, the picture of the Gnostic redeemer drew the heart of its picture outside the dots we have. It was a pretty picture, but it required us to hypothesize the existence of a lot of dots that weren't there.

> Hypotheses are pictures we draw out of the dots that are available to us. A good hypothesis sticks closely to the available dots and forms the heart of its picture from them.

I personally believe that future scholars will look back at some recent trends in the study of Jesus with a similar puzzlement. It is true that a comparison of the four gospel presentations of Jesus in detail raises a number of questions about how it really happened and what was really said. Even if it is possible in the end to fit these portraits together on a historical level, they do at times give us quite different "feels." If we had stood there on the countryside, would we have experienced Jesus as the mysterious, yet very human individual of Mark or the very openly divine person of John?

Thus for well over a hundred years scholars have drawn a potential distinction between the "historical Jesus" and Jesus as the gospels portray him. This distinction has given rise to the so-called quest for the historical Jesus, the quest for who Jesus really was, what he really said, and what he really did. Solutions to the quest vary. On the one end of the spectrum are those who think that the gospels basically give us Jesus as he really was, even if the gospels each come at him from a different vantage point. On the other end of the spectrum are those who believe it is impossible to know anything about the historical Jesus at all and that the real Jesus is lost to history.

One paradigm for understanding Jesus that has recently gained a significant following basically sees Jesus as a teacher of popular wisdom. This perspective, best represented by a group of scholars called the Jesus Seminar, argues that Jesus did not see himself as a messiah and that he did not teach anything about God's approaching judgment or his eventual return to earth. These scholars have little confidence in the gospel portraits as we now have them. Instead, they sift through the gospel material, as well as through other documents about Jesus from the ancient world.

I personally believe that future scholarship will view this paradigm in much the same way we now view the Gnostic Redeemer myth. Like the Gnostic paradigm, the Jesus Seminar constructs a view largely on the basis of later sources and hypothetical sources. Thus they look to later writings like the *Gospel of Thomas* and the *Gospel of Peter.* It is certainly possible that these writings have incorporated earlier material in them, but the *Gospel of Thomas* in particular shows influences that are much later than Jesus. In other words, I think later scholars will agree that these writings have little new to tell us than what we already have in the New Testament gospels.

This portrait of Jesus also draws heavily on a hypothetical reconstruction of a source used by Matthew and Luke. If you remember from above, most scholars believe that Mark was written first and that Matthew and Luke have used it to provide the skeleton of their gospels. But we go on to notice that Matthew and Luke also have a great deal of teaching material in common that is often worded similarly. Scholars have often suggested that both of them were drawing on another common source for this material, material that is sometimes called "Q" after the German word for "source."

Of course we have no copies of this document—if it even was a written source. The idea of its existence is plausible enough. But when we begin to talk about stages in its development or the community that produced it, we are getting more and more hypothetical. I personally am not opposed to asking questions like these, but clearly we are swimming farther and farther out into uncertain waters.

And it is in these waters that we find the Q of the Jesus Seminar. It is a place where all the teaching of Jesus relating to God's coming judgment and Christ's role in it has been stripped away. I want to be careful here. I don't feel that we can just dismiss all of the criteria and methods the Seminar used to arrive at its conclusions. But in the end I feel that other more obvious features of Jesus' life and message prevail.

While the Jesus Seminar represents a very significant portion of Jesus scholarship at the moment, we can also observe another segment of the guild that argues strongly for a Jesus who saw himself in messianic terms and who preached the coming judgment of God.[14] While the Jesus seminar focused on the *words* of Jesus, proponents of this more messianic Jesus focus equally on the *events* of Jesus' life. As an aside we see again the immense flexibility that words in themselves have and how they need to be grounded in something beyond themselves!

Everyone agrees that Jesus was probably baptized by John the Baptist— why would anyone make up a story that put him in a subordinate position to

John? Yet we know both from the New Testament and the Jewish historian Josephus that John preached the renewal of Israel, that God was doing something in history. When Jesus was baptized by John, he assented to what John was doing. Here is our first objective hint that Jesus saw himself as part of something God was doing in history, not just as a wise teacher.

Most agree that Jesus appointed twelve disciples, even if there are some tensions in the gospels as to what the exact names of the twelve were. Twelve is a highly suggestive number, as it was the number of the tribes of Israel. In other words, it seems to suggest some agenda for Israel beyond simply wise teaching. Yet Jesus did not consider himself as one of the twelve, which probably means he thought he had an even greater role. Could he have thought that he was the messiah?

We could present other evidence both from likely events and sayings that point toward a Jesus who

> The next generation of scholars may look back at the current scholarly paradigms in puzzlement.

believed that God was on the verge of doing something fantastic in history and that he stood at the very center of it. To those who are new to these kinds of discussions, these comments will seem like understatements. Of course Jesus did; he was God. My point is not to deny these aspects of our Christian faith.

My point is to show how paradigms influence even those who know the most about the evidence. Even the best scholars are affected by the glasses they wear. Paradigms come and go. New evidence is discovered, and a whole generation re-examines the biblical texts in its light. I am optimistic that we know a great deal about the original meaning of the Bible. But the next generation of scholars may also look back at my paradigms in wonder.

The complexity of the preceding discussion may amaze you. Your jaw may be hanging open to realize how extensively scholars debate issues you have never heard about. This fact brings us back once again to the question of relevance. If we must reach some degree of certainty on all these things, if we need to know about these issues to understand the original meaning, isn't the vast majority of Christendom in trouble? Isn't there a more excellent way?

---

[1] W. W. Klein, C. L. Blomberg, and R. L. Hubbard, *An Introduction to Biblical Interpretation* (Nashville: Nelson, 1993).

[2] *Biblical Interpretation*, 406-424.

[3] Full English publication: J. D. G. Dunn, ed., *Paul and the Mosaic Law: Durham-Tübingen Research Symposium on Earliest Christianity and Judaism* (Grand Rapids: Eerdmans, 2001).

[4] So B. M. Foschini, "'Those Who Are Baptized for the Dead,' I Cor. 15:29, An Exegetical Historical Dissertation," *Catholic Biblical Quarterly* 12 (1950): 260.

[5] So G. D. Fee, *The First Epistle to the Corinthians* (Grand Rapids: Eerdmans, 1987), 261.

[6] And after all, Jesus taught in Aramaic rather than Greek, so we would still have the phenomenon of three translations being almost verbatim at various points. Further, at least Mark and Luke were not eyewitnesses of Jesus' ministry. Only John actually claims to come from an eyewitness, the unidentified "beloved disciple" (John 21:24). Of course none of the four gospels actually tells us the name of its author. The titles were added later, decades after the gospels were written.

[7] As K. E. Bailey has put it, "informal, controlled tradition" ("Informal Controlled Oral Tradition and the Synoptic Gospels," *Asia Journal of Theology* 5 [1991]: 34-54).

[8] Thus J. D. G. Dunn, *Jesus Remembered* (Grand Rapids: Eerdmans, 2003), 222.

[9] The ground breaking article in this regard was that of K. Stendahl, "The Apostle Paul and the Introspective Conscience of the West," *HTR* 56 (1963): 199-215.

[10] If we read Romans 7:7-24 in context, that is, as the unfolding of the content of 7:5, we realize that these verses must apply to what the Romans "were" when they were in the flesh. If we do not move on from Romans 7 to Romans 8, which expands on 7:6, we drastically misconstrue what Paul was saying.

[11] A truth generally ignored by scholars of the early twentieth century as "naughty data," despite the well argued protests of individuals like G. F. Moore and W. D. Davies. The decisive turning point on this issue came with the work of E. P. Sanders, *Paul and Palestinian Judaism: A Comparison of Patterns of Religion* (Philadelphia: Fortress, 1977).

[12] Sanders's famous distinction.

[13] E.g., S. Kim, *Paul and the New Perspective: Second Thoughts on the Origin of Paul's Gospel* (Grand Rapids: Eerdmans, 2002).

[14] Two of the main proponents of this view, each in their own way, are E. P. Sanders, *Jesus and Judaism* (Philadelphia: Fortress, 1985) and N. T. Wright, *Jesus and the Victory of God* (Minneapolis: Fortress, 1996).

Chapter 5
When the Spirit in the Church Decides

More than the Bible

The Church of England, the Anglican Church, has always straddled the fence between catholicism and Protestantism. On the one hand, it withdrew from the Roman Catholic Church in the 1500's like other Protestant groups in Europe did. The trigger for its withdrawal was the desire of King Henry VIII for a divorce—and the Pope's refusal to grant it. Neither side was particularly virtuous in the matter, for the Pope at that time might have granted the divorce if the woman in question had not been the daughter of the King of Spain, a king who happened to be breathing down his neck at the time.

Yet Henry VIII himself had earlier written a treatise against Martin Luther, the father of the Reformation and Protestantism. Henry was thus not your ordinary Protestant. Anglicans like John Jewel would argue in the following years that the Church of England was still catholic—just not *Roman* Catholic.[1] The Orthodox tradition in Greece, Russia, and the east make similar claims to be catholic churches, small c. Groups like these view the Roman Catholic Church as a part of this broader catholicism, just not the exclusive bearer of the tradition.[2]

One feature these catholic groups have in common is the greater role they are willing to acknowledge the traditions of the church play alongside Scripture. While they all consider Scripture a very important element in the equation, perhaps even the focal point of the equation, other elements are equally crucial. At times of course this approach has led to periods where the Bible played little role in the life of such churches. But we would be wrong to think such was always the case. The Roman Catholic Church of today has a high reverence for Scripture, as do Orthodox churches. Mark Noll has recently made it clear that it is increasingly difficult to distinguish between Protestant and Catholic in the way they use the Bible.[3]

Martin Luther protested against several aspects of the Roman Catholic Church of his day, particularly with regard to traditions that went well beyond the teaching of the Bible. For example, he rejected the insistence of the Roman Catholic Church that priests be celibate. He rejected the idea of purgatory as an intermediate place for the dead—dead individuals who were destined for heaven but not yet pure enough to go there. He especially rejected the idea that you could get out of purgatory sooner by donating money to the Church.

Many of Luther's reforms were no doubt needed in the Roman Catholic Church of his day. After all, Rome itself "cleaned house" in the years that followed.[4] However, as is so often the case, Luther set in motion a reaction that would become an over-reaction. The Reformation principle, "Scripture only," began a process that has since fragmented Christianity into tens of thousands of little groups who all think they know what Scripture alone teaches. Yet they all disagree with one another at many points.

In the end, the Bible alone can *never* be the sole source of Christian authority. It is an impossibility of language, particularly when it comes to the language of the Bible. All language needs a context for its meaning to become fixed, and the books of the Bible in themselves presuppose dozens of such contexts. And all these contexts themselves are ancient rather than contemporary. Until evangelical and fundamentalists churches recognize these basic truths, there will never be a real understanding between Christians.

We will see in this chapter that Christian tradition has always played a role in the legitimate appropriation of Scripture.[5] Those who interpret the Bible without regard for Christian traditions inevitably end up founding cults like that of David Koresh. From reformers like Martin Luther and John Calvin in the

1500's to the conservative evangelicals of today, legitimate biblical interpretation has always drawn on Christian tradition as a guide in biblical interpretation.

John Wesley, the founder of Methodism, provides us with a good Protestant model for redressing the

> Christian tradition has always played a role in the legitimate appropriation of Scripture.

excesses of the Protestant Reformation. Certainly the eighteenth century Wesley sounded like he was just as convinced in the idea of "Scripture alone" as any other reformer when he was challenging the Roman Catholic Church.[6] But his roots in the Anglican Church led him in practice to resort to tradition, experience, and even reason in his appropriation of the Bible for his day.

Wesley's method of appropriating Scripture is sometimes called "Wesley's Quadrilateral," although Wesley himself didn't come up with the term.[7] The idea is that while Scripture is the central and determinative element in the equation; tradition, reason, and experience also are valid sources of truth. If you would, they are filters through which we pass the Bible's teaching. For example, some in the Wesleyan tradition have used this quadrilateral as a model for determining God's will for your life. You ask if your course of action fits with Scripture, with what other Christians have said and are saying about it (traditions), with your experiences and the experiences of others, and with common sense (reason).[8]

> Human reasoning and experience are always factors in our appropriation of the Bible. They are the "round house" through which all the trains of knowledge pass.

Our pilgrimage through this book requires us to modify the Wesleyan Quadrilateral slightly. One observation we have made throughout is that our thoughts and experiences are *always* an inevitable element in biblical interpretation. In other words, human reasoning and experience are always factors in our appropriation of the Bible. They are the "round house" through which all the trains of knowledge pass. We can do nothing else; here is how it stands.

When we ask what the Bible's meaning is, we are thinking. If the Holy Spirit speaks to me, I am experiencing something and then filtering that experience through my reflection. I have to connect the teaching of one part of Scripture with that of the others. In short, it is never Scripture alone determining its meaning. The most determinative factors in the meaning I see are *outside* the text, elements I bring with me to the text.

We are at an excellent point in history to redress the imbalances of the Protestant Reformation both on the Roman Catholic and Protestant sides. It is time for us Protestants to own up to the fact that tradition has played as great a role in our appropriation of Scripture as the words of Scripture itself. Not to own up to this fact creates a situation in which we allow random interpretations to go unchecked with the authority of God.

At the same time, it seems difficult to think of all the developments throughout the history of the church as some straightforward evolution. Must all ministers be celibate today because the church of the late Middle Ages insisted on celibacy? We always seem to run aground on the shore of persecution and excess when God's church is mistaken for any one political church entity. Somehow we need to allow for mistakes and passing phases in history.

This chapter asks how we can discern the unfolding of God's revelation in Scripture and in the traditions of Christians throughout the ages. We are especially interested in how those traditions have influenced the way we read Scripture. We can be sure that God's Spirit is the ultimate source of all such truth. Surely the Spirit speaks both to individuals and to communities of faith.

But we are on safest ground when we are reading the Bible in communities of faith.[9] The more Christians, the more likely we are truly hearing the Spirit. We can draw this principle out: we are most likely of all to hear God's Spirit when we are in the "communion of saints" throughout the ages. If God's Spirit lives in the body of Christ, made up of all Christians in all times and places, then it is when we are in fellowship with the church of the ages that we are most likely to hear God's Spirit on any particular belief or practice.

Rebuilding Our Faith in the Church

The way the Protestant tradition has sometimes downplayed the significance of the church and Christian tradition is deeply ironic in some respects. For example, we

> If God's Spirit lives in the body of Christ, then it is when we are in fellowship with the church of the ages that we are most likely to hear God's Spirit on any particular belief or practice.

would not have a New Testament if God had not worked through the church to collect and recognize the authority of its books. We would not have a New Testament if there had not been a church. We would only have individual books that various Christians used.

> We would not have a New Testament if there had not been a church to collect and recognize the authority of its books.

We are not talking about some political body or denomination here when we speak of "the church." Rather, we are referring to everyone whom God has claimed as his own by placing his Spirit on them (2 Corinthians 5:5). It's not important for us to define the precise boundaries of the church here, other than to say that the church overlaps significantly with all those who have considered themselves Christians throughout the ages. Surely we do not find the true church in some small, relatively obscure group that has the truth all to its own. The universal church is ultimately "invisible" and has existed since the days of Christ.[10] Only God knows for sure who is truly in it and who is not.

If we have faith in the Bible, then we must have faith that God worked through the Christians of the first few centuries to "ratify" which books were authoritative enough to be considered Scripture. Remember, each of these books was written individually at a different time and place. They only became an authoritative collection because the church came to affirm their authority. The books of the Bible are thus sometimes referred to as the "canon," from a

Greek word that has the sense of a measuring rod. In other words, these are the books against which Christians should measure themselves.

On the one hand, most Christians agreed on the bulk of these books within a century of when they were written. The books themselves came into existence over at least a fifty year period, starting with the letters of Paul in the 50's and extending at least until Revelation in the 90's.[11] They were written in various locations across the Mediterranean world, so a process of collection ensued in the decades that followed.

By the end of the 100's, the four gospels, Acts, and the letters of Paul were probably considered Scripture by most Christians. Of course there were also other groups like the Gnostic Christians who had any number of gospels that they produced and considered authoritative. But these groups and their writings did not stand the test of time. If we adopt the model of the Spirit working through the church of the ages, we wonder if the ultimate extinction of these groups shows that God did not ultimately want their form of Christianity to be *the* form. We may find many of them in the kingdom of God, but the Spirit did not lead the church in their direction.

While the bulk of the New Testament found relatively early consensus, some of the other books faced lengthy debate. Hebrews, James, 2 Peter, Revelation—these books had their proponents and their detractors. 1 Clement, the Shepherd of Hermas, the Apocalypse of Peter—these books also had their proponents and detractors. The ones that look familiar to you are the ones the church ultimately came to consider Scripture. Not that the church necessarily thought the others were bad books—they just did not ultimately assign them as much authority as the other ones.

It is interesting that the contours of the New Testament canon were not set by a church council or meeting.[12] In other words, the canon was not really set by a vote.[13] Certainly there were political figures involved, but the church managed to reach a general consensus on the canon without the kinds of debates it had on issues like the divinity of Christ. The first instance (we know of) when someone suggested the precise list of books we now call the New Testament was in AD367 in the Easter letter of a man by the name of Athanasius. While some debate continued in the century thereafter, this suggestion seemed to resonate with the church. Aside from some early misgivings by Martin Luther, the church has not questioned this list ever since.[14] If we are to have faith in the Bible, we must have faith that God was working in the minds of Christians to lead them to this list. God did so despite some apparent misunderstandings these early Christians had.

For example, you will search long and hard to find an original meaning scholar of the Bible who thinks that the apostle Paul wrote the book of Hebrews. Yet the acceptance of Hebrews into the canon coincides largely with the belief that Paul was its author. Apparently God wanted it in and brought it in, working around the misconceptions of the Christians involved.

The "Scripture alone" position thus finds itself in a "chicken and egg" situation: which came first, Scripture or the church? While the individual

> Those who believe that the books in our Bibles are authoritative must at least believe that God worked in the church beyond the New Testament in this one area.

books of the Bible came first, they did not become "authoritative Scripture" without the church. Those who believe that the books in our Bibles are authoritative must at least believe that God worked in the church beyond the New Testament in this one area. But if he worked in the church on this issue, isn't it just possible that he has been working in the church on other important items as well?

Development within the Bible

If we believe that the Bible is a model for how God reveals truth to his people, then perhaps the Bible itself has something to say on this issue. Did God ever unfold truth over a long period of time between the books of the Bible? Did he sometimes tailor his revelation for particular times and places? Indeed, we do see such development of belief in the course of the Bible, particularly in the time between the Old and the New Testament.

> The Bible itself models the idea that God sometimes unfolds his revelation over long periods of time and even tailors it for particular phases of history.

For example, the bulk of the Old Testament has no real sense of a personal, conscious afterlife. On the contrary, the psalmist says, "Turn, O LORD, preserve my life; save me because of your faithfulness. For there is no remembrance of you in death; in Sheol who gives praise to you?" (Psalm 6:4-5). Similarly, Ecclesiastes says that "the fate of the sons of man and the fate of the animal—it is one fate. The death of the one is like the death of the other, and there is one spirit [breath] to all ... All go to one place" (Ecclesiastes 3:19-20).[15]

The only place in the entire Old Testament where we find undisputed teaching on the afterlife is in the book of Daniel. And even here it is not clear that everyone will experience it: "Many who sleep in the dust of the ground will awake, some to everlasting life, and some to reproach and everlasting disgrace" (Daniel 12:2). The vast majority of the Old Testament, not to mention all Jewish literature thereafter until around 200BC, has no real concept of the afterlife.

The situation could not be more different when we come to the New Testament. The entirety of the New Testament assumes the reality of the afterlife, particularly a future resurrection in which our bodies return to life in some sort of transformed state (e.g., 1 Corinthians 15). If we are to maintain our Christian beliefs, we must conclude that God turned on the lights of revelation in the time between the two testaments with regard to this issue. In other words, we witness a development in understanding within the pages of the Bible itself.

An even more fascinating example of such development takes place in the time between the writing of 2 Samuel 24:1 and 1 Chronicles 21:1. 2 Samuel 24:1 reads, "The anger of *the* LORD increasingly burned against Israel, and he incited David against them..." In contrast, the later book 2 Chronicles reads,

"*Satan* stood against Israel, and incited David..." The contrast is shocking: Chronicles says that Satan did something that Samuel says God did!

The difference is that between 2 Samuel and 1 Chronicles, some Jews had come to accept the concept of a Satan, a heavenly figure who tested people's loyalty to God. Thus in Job we see the Satan testing Job and reporting back to God (Job 1:6-12; 2:1-7). Before Israel had gone into captivity, they spoke of God as the cause of both the good and the bad things that happened to them. But after Israel returned from Babylon, many of them would now think of Satan as the direct cause of such bad things.

But even at this point the Jews did not think of Satan as an evil angel who stood in diametric opposition to God. The Satan of Job and Chronicles still works under God. It is not until around the time of Christ that we find a Jewish writing equating the serpent of Genesis with Satan.[16] Here is another good example of a new "definition" some parts of the New Testament bring to the words of the Old Testament that was not the original definition.[17] Genesis itself does not mention Satan. It is the New Testament that leads us to understand the serpent as Satan. We must conclude again that God turned on the lights of revelation on this issue over time and that the Bible demonstrates a development in understanding within its own pages.

We can also recognize that the New Testament sometimes reverses or changes the direction of the Old Testament. We have already seen such a change in our earlier discussion of the Sabbath.[18] The Old Testament assumes the importance of the Sabbath. In fact, Israel stoned a man to death for gathering sticks on the Sabbath (Numbers 15:32-36). But for whatever reason, the New Testament condemns someone who would require a non-Jewish Christian to keep the Sabbath (Colossians 2:16; Romans 14:5-6).

Another example of such a reversal is Jesus' teaching on divorce. The Old Testament places no restrictions on divorce but assumes it (e.g., Deuteronomy 24:1). Indeed, the books of Ezra and Nehemiah tell of a time when those Jews who had married foreign wives were commanded to divorce their foreign wives and children (Ezra 10:3). Yet Jesus says, "It was because you were so hard-hearted that Moses allowed you to divorce your wives" (Matthew 19:8). In other words, God sometimes allows his people to do less than his ideal—even in his biblical instruction.

We must apparently accept that God sometimes unfolds his revelation over long periods of time, for we can

> God sometimes gave instruction in the Bible that accommodated particular audiences—even though it wasn't his ideal.

witness this process within the pages of the Bible itself. And even in the Bible God sometimes gave instruction that accommodated particular audiences—even though it was not his ideal. We have certainly seen time and time again that God more often than not revealed biblical truth within the categories of his audiences. The crucial question now is whether God continued these processes beyond the pages of the New Testament and into the church, perhaps even to today.

Development beyond the Bible

Can we identify beliefs that are essential to Christian faith as we know it, yet that are not clearly taught in Scripture? Are there even things we accept today that even conflict with the biblical categories, but that we have not allowed ourselves to admit because we want to base our beliefs exclusively on the Bible without recourse to the church? More than any other, this is the most crucial question of this book.

Our beliefs about Christ seem to provide us with an important test case. Are the things we believe about Jesus clearly taught in the New Testament or are many of them beliefs that ultimately come from Christian tradition about Jesus? Certainly the early church debated vigorously the exact nature of Christ's humanity and divinity. Was Jesus fully human, or only somewhat human? Is Jesus divine in the same way as God the Father or only in a similar way? Are God the Father and God the Son in fact the same person? If not, do Christians believe in one God, two Gods, or maybe even three Gods?

I would argue that the books of the New Testament did not settle these issues. Indeed, I would argue that the New Testament at times lent its support more to the arguments of people we now think of as heretics than to those who supported what we now believe. I do not make this claim to undermine what we currently believe. On the contrary, I am presuming that God has brought his people to believe the right things about Jesus. What I am arguing is that God brought the church to affirm these things *after* the New Testament—that the development of Christian doctrine and ethics continued beyond the pages of the Bible.

> God brought the church to affirm a number of things about Christ *after* the New Testament.

The New International Version (NIV) provides us with several great case studies on this subject, because its translations often mirror evangelical theology. Nowhere is this more apparent than in the way it translates certain key passages about Christ. Thus the NIV translates Philippians 2:6 in this way: Jesus, "being in very nature God, did not consider equality with God something to be grasped." When it translates the verse this way, it supports the Christian belief that Jesus was fully God in his nature. The Council of Nicaea in 325 affirmed that although God exists in three persons (Father, Son, and Holy Spirit), he is only one God consisting of one substance.

The NIV similarly translates Colossians 1:15 in the following way: Jesus "is the image of the invisible God, the firstborn over all creation." By translating the last phrase "firstborn *over* all creation," the NIV avoids the impression that Jesus is a part of the creation—he is not the firstborn *of* all creation. This way of translating the verse assists us in holding to another conclusion of the Council of Nicaea: Jesus was "eternally begotten of the Father, begotten, not made."[19] The Council denied the claims of a man named Arius, who believed that Christ was the first thing that God created.

I would argue that the NIV is an excellent *Christian* translation at these points in the sense that it facilitates a Christian reading of these verses. But I would argue it ultimately does so because of the influence of legitimate Christian tradition, in particular the influence of the world-wide councils of the church's first few centuries. The Council of Nicaea in 325 affirmed that God is a Trinity: he is one God consisting of one substance while also in some mysterious way being three persons—Father, Son, and Holy Spirit. The Council of Chalcedon in 451 affirmed that Jesus was both fully human and fully divine, one person with two natures. These are things that Christians throughout the ages have believed, both Protestant and Catholic. An individual or group that does not believe them has some serious explaining to do.

Yet I would argue that the NIV has not rendered these verses strictly in terms of their original meanings—it has taken some interpretive liberty in the light of later Christian tradition. Thus the New Revised Standard Version (NRSV) renders Philippians 2:6 more literally: Jesus, "though he was in the form of God, did not regard equality with God as something to be exploited." There is a significant jump from the phrase "form of God" in the Greek to the NIV's "being in very nature God." As you might suspect, the Greek original has given rise to an immense body of scholarly literature. Some think the phrase "form of God" only means that Jesus was like Adam, who was made in the image of God (Genesis 1:27). In contrast, most scholars think it referred to Jesus as pre-existent in some way.

With so much ink spilled over this verse, I could not hope to convince anyone of *my* understanding in a paragraph, not even in a scholarly article or book. It is indeed possible that it refers to Christ's existence before he was born, although this interpretation is not nearly as clear to me as it is to many others. More significantly, I notice that "form of God" is in contrast to "form of a servant" and think it is much more about the royal status of Christ than about some aspect of his nature.[20] In the end, I just want you to see how helpful the judgment of the later church was in nailing down our beliefs on the pre-existent Christ. In a very real sense, we don't have to worry about the original meaning of this verse because God has settled what we are to believe about Christ through the church.

The NIV's translation of Colossians 1:15 is even more to the point. Again, the NRSV gives us a less interpreted translation: Jesus "is the image of the invisible God, the firstborn of all creation." A Christian named Arius argued strongly in the early 300's that this verse implied that Christ was, in the end, created by God and not "of the same substance" as God the Father. He believed that Christ was the firstborn *of* God's creations. Arius would have agreed that Christ was "over all creation" as well, that Christ was pre-eminent over everything except God. But he believed that God made Christ and thus that there was a point at which Christ had not existed.

Enter another man named Athanasius. He argued strongly not only that Christ had existed from all eternity, but that he was of the same substance as God the Father. The church came to conclude that Christ was not less than God in any way. Athanasius would not even accept the compromise that Christ was of a *similar* substance to God the Father. He must be of the *same* substance. While the debate continued long and heavy after the confrontation between Arius and Athanasius, Christians eventually came to accept Athanasius' view. And this is what we Christians believe today.

But notice that the New Testament doesn't come anywhere near to asking these questions, let alone to answering them. When Paul says, "The grace of the Lord Jesus Christ and the love of God and the fellowship of the Holy Spirit be with you all," he mentions all three persons of the Trinity. But he never gives us anything like a statement on how these three relate to each other— especially a statement like we now believe. The bottom line is that the New Testament alone was not able to settle these crucial debates in Christian history. The original meaning of the Bible alone is not yet fully Christian in the sense that it could not arbitrate between what we now consider heresy and orthodoxy.

In the end, Arius' interpretation may have fit better with Colossians' original meaning than Athanasius'. The language of Colossians is very similar to language that some Jews of that day used to talk about God's word, his *logos*. We know that early Jewish Christians drew on these traditions because the Gospel of John uses the

> The New Testament alone could not settle the great Trinitarian and Christological debates of the 300's and 400's. Its original meaning was insufficient to arbitrate between the major options of these debates.

same language: "In the beginning was the Word [*logos*]" (John 1:1). These Jewish traditions considered God's word to be God's firstborn son too, "neither uncreated as God, nor created as you, but midway."[21] In other words, while they gave supremacy to God's word, they still placed it on the created side of the line. Since the New Testament used this imagery without objecting to this aspect of it, it seems likely that the New Testament authors did not take issue with the idea that Christ was created. It was not an issue that came up on their radar.

We see also that the New Testament places Christ beneath God: "Whenever he subjects all things to him [Christ], then the Son himself will also be subjected to the one who subjected all things to him, so that God might be all in all" (1 Corinthians 15:28). To be sure, Christians like Athanasius had ways of reinterpreting verses like these to fit with the idea of the Trinity. For example, some argued that it was only the human side of Christ that would be subordinated to God the father. His divine nature would of course remain equal with God as it was for all time. But we have once again moved into questions that lie well beyond those of the New Testament.

In all these cases it is of course *possible* to argue that the traditional beliefs of the church are in fact the original meanings of these verses. Evangelical scholars interpret the Bible this way all the time so that they can maintain the sense that they do not rely on Christian tradition for their beliefs, only the Bible. But time and time again we can seriously question whether they are coming up with the most *probable* interpretations in terms of the original meaning. It would be deeply ironic if a desire to make the original meaning of the Bible the ultimate source of what we believe repeatedly led to playing games with the original meaning, forcing it to agree with beliefs that are absolutely legitimate, but that really come from God's inspiration of the church beyond the pages of the Bible.

Ironically, the desire to make the original meaning of the Bible the ultimate source of what we believe repeatedly leads some scholars to play games with the original meaning. Such scholars force their interpretations to agree with absolutely legitimate beliefs that really come from God's inspiration of the church beyond the pages of the Bible.

Do we really need to argue that these interpretations of Paul's writings are the *original* meanings in order for us to accept them as valid *Christian* appropriations of these words? Indeed, it seems more likely in these instances that the original meaning must take second place to the beliefs God has led Christians everywhere to affirm and hold for over 1500 years. Is it in fact the cultural presuppositions of our age that presumes the authority of Scripture must lie in the original, historical meaning of a passage? We saw in the previous chapter that if we have to know the original meaning to find God's voice, most Christians throughout the ages are in trouble. Is it possible that God more uses the words of Bible as a mirror in which the church sees itself and the directions in which God is leading it?

We can see this contrast of perspective in the different translations of the New Testament. Most Christians today have no problem at all with what we might call "modern" translations of the Bible. Yet some will still remember a time when some Christians fought tooth and nail for the King James Version (KJV) as the only valid English Bible. Certainly we can understand why someone raised on the KJV might be surprised to come upon statements like the following: "The earliest manuscripts and some other ancient witnesses do not have Mark 16:9-20."[22] If you had grown up reading these verses as part of the Bible, you would immediately suspect that some faithless person was tampering with Scripture.

But the background to this debate is the fact that the Greek text behind the KJV was edited in the 1400's and 1500's when the oldest copies of the New Testament we had dated to the Middle Ages. Since then we have discovered substantial manuscripts of the New Testament that go back to the 200's and 300's. These earlier manuscripts generally agree with the later ones, but there are some exceptions. The ending of the Gospel of Mark is a case in point. We have good reason to believe that this ending did not really start appearing in copies of Mark until the 300's.

The historical orientation of our culture has generally led Christians, including Christian scholars, to assume that what we need to do is "get back" to the original text. This drive is similar to the drive to get back to the original meaning of the Bible or to get back to the "historical" Jesus. Accordingly, nearly all modern translations follow the earlier text of the New Testament simply because it is indeed more original than the Greek text behind the King James.

But consider our discussion of relevance in the previous chapter. It is not the original text that Christians used from the 400's till the 1800's—it was the "church's text" that served as the basis of the King James. This text must not have been too faulty, for God didn't object to its use. Indeed, this text makes clearer some of the Christian beliefs that crystallized in the first centuries of the church. It is the text we find in the vast majority of handwritten copies of the New Testament. It is not the original text, but it is the church's.

By and large it has not been the original meaning that has spoken to countless Christians throughout the ages. Thus Christians have consistently read the Old Testament with Christian eyes rather than in terms of its original meaning. Indeed, the Greek Orthodox Church does not even consider the original Hebrew Old Testament to be Scripture. Rather, their Old Testament is the later Greek translation of the Old Testament that the New Testament used as its Bible.[23] It is a text that fit with early Christian beliefs about Christ more easily than the original Hebrew text did.

We have now seen that Christians also read the New Testament with the eyes of Christian traditions about the nature of Christ. These beliefs were hammered out in the first few centuries of the church—they were not the debates or issues of the New Testament authors themselves. In many cases these beliefs force the original meaning of the Bible into a subordinate role in the formulation of our faith. They illustrate that God continued to unfold revelation in the lives of his people beyond the pages of the New Testament.

Balancing Continuity with Change

This sense of development in the church leaves us with many questions. Did such development end with the early councils of the church? If we did not stop with the New Testament, it seems hard to stop with the first five world-wide councils. But I prefer not to think of such development in terms of the decisions of political bodies. There were councils whose decisions we do not hear of today, because their conclusions did not stand the test of time.[24]

Thus Christians everywhere have come to recognize that the institution of slavery is ultimately incompatible with the essence of Christian faith.

> God's movement in the church is patient. Sometimes he accommodates the hard-heartedness of generations. Sometimes he meets cultures with context-specific beliefs and practices.

We cannot point to any universal council where this idea was ratified. It bubbled up from the Spirit speaking in the church. By faith I believe that the same process is currently at work with regard to women in ministry and in the home. I suspect in two hundred years even the Roman Catholic Church will have women priests! It simply violates our spiritual common sense to suggest that women are spiritually inferior to men in any way.

God's movement in this manner is patient. He has shown no hurry in reaching these destinations. For centuries he can show a willingness to accommodate the hard-hearts of generation after generation, just as he did in the Old Testament with regard to divorce. No doubt there are eras during which God meets various cultures and contexts with particular understandings that are not meant to endure but that nevertheless meet the needs of those times and places. We must always allow for prophets among us who lead us in directions that only become consensus generations later.

And while I have sharply criticized the idea that the original meaning is the "be all and end all" of the Bible, I believe it also has a role to play. Once we know how to read the Bible in context, it becomes more difficult to hear God's voice by random words ripped out of their context. Even though scholarly paradigms can change, God meets us in the categories we have, "stooping to our weakness."[25] So even when our understanding of the original meaning turns out to have problems, God can speak to us where we are at in our understanding.

And ultimately I believe we can conclude many true things about the original meaning. If these understandings are true and God is a God of truth, then surely they also become a factor in how God moves the church forward. In other words, the original meaning can become a part of the way God's Spirit speaks to the church. If we are allowing for passing phases in the thinking and practice of Christianity, then perhaps at times God uses scholars like Martin Luther to redirect traditions that have departed from the original meaning in inappropriate ways.

> We recognize God's movement best when we look back at the Spirit's working in the church over time.

It would seem that we recognize God's movement best when we look back at the Spirit's working in the church over time. We can never be absolutely certain where he is leading in our own day. But if the Spirit of God lives in the entire body of Christ, then we are on safest ground when we are in dialog with the early church through the Scriptures, the church of the ages through tradition, as well as the visible church of today.

Guiding Principle 2: Interpretation within the Faith of the Church

We arrived at the first guiding principle for biblical interpretation in chapter three. Any interpretation that fits with our love of God and our fellow human is an appropriate interpretation of the Bible—whether it is the original meaning or not. This guiding principle relates primarily on how we use the Bible when we are trying to know how to live out our lives in this world.

We are now ready to supplement our guidelines with a rule of thumb for questions about what we should believe. Here the guiding principle is that our beliefs need to fit with the beliefs that God has "bubbled up" into the church through the Holy Spirit. Any interpretation that fits with the faith of the church throughout the ages is an appropriate interpretation. This is true even if those interpretations are not the original meanings the Bible had.

To avoid the pitfalls we have witnessed so often in history, it seems we must also allow for prophets who challenge the

> Any interpretation that fits with the faith of the church throughout the ages is an appropriate interpretation whether it is the original meaning or not.

prevailing views of the church as well. But we should not be too ready to accept such challenges. If they do speak for God's Spirit, rarely will we see the church as a whole move in their direction until long after they are dead. This process may seem puzzling to us. Why does God work in this way? The answer that makes the most sense to me is that it is because God truly cares for us. He is more concerned with meeting us where we are than with making sure he gets his due.

---

[1] I thank Father Neil Evans for his insights into John Jewel, who along with Cardinal John Newman were important stops in his ecclesiastical pilgrimage from the Anglican to the Roman Catholic Church.

[2] They are sometimes even willing to consider the Pope, the "bishop of Rome," as the "first among equals."

[3] *Is the Reformation Over?: An Evangelical Assessment of Contemporary Roman Catholicism* (Grand Rapids: Baker Academic, 2005).

[4] The so-called Counter Reformation, which of course also involved an attempt to force Protestants to get in line.

[5] For a good start toward this realization, see Daniel H. Williams, *Evangelicals And Tradition: The Formative Influence Of The Early Church* (Grand Rapids: Baker Academic, 2005).

[6] E.g., in his essay, "A Roman Catechism, faithfully drawn out of the allowed writings of the Church of Rome: With a Reply thereto."

[7] Coined by A. C. Outler in his book *John Wesley* (Oxford: Oxford University, 1981).

[8] M. W. Knapp, the cofounder of a holiness group in the early 1900's, played out this approach in a book titled *Impressions*.

[9] Several recent books are moving in this same direction. One notable one is S. E. Fowl and L. G. Jones's *Reading in Communion: Scripture and Ethics in Christian Life* (Grand Rapids: Eerdmans, 1991).

[10] By "invisible," I simply mean we cannot equate the church with any visible group or denomination like the Roman Catholic Church. By contrast, as the *body* of Christ in which the Spirit dwells, the true church always involves collections of visible bodies, not lone individuals off by themselves.

[11] Many scholars would date books like 2 Peter even later.

[12] You sometimes hear people say that the Council of Nicaea in 325 set the canon, but this is incorrect. There was a Council in Carthage in 397 that affirmed the current list, but this was not a universal council.

[13] The issue is more complicated with regard to the Old Testament. If we go by the use of the church, including hints we get from the New Testament church, the canon of the Old Testament would at least give some status to the books in the Roman Catholic Old Testament. The same Council of Carthage mentioned in the previous note afforded Scriptural status to the books Protestants now call the Apocrypha as well as to the ones Protestant now use. Roman Church actually made the broader Old Testament canon official in 1545 at the Council of Trent in reaction to Luther, who rejected these writings. We cannot currently speak of consensus on this issue.

[14] Luther at first did not translate James or Revelation into German. At the time he thought of James as an "epistle of straw."

[15] Other similar passages include Job 7:9-10; 14:14, 20-22; Psalms 30:9; 88:10-11; Isaiah 38:18.

[16] *The Life of Adam and Eve*, perhaps from the first century BC.

[17] E.g., Romans 16:20; 2 Corinthians 11:3; Hebrews 2:14; Revelation 12:9; 20:2.

[18] In chapter 3.

[19] A line from the Nicene Creed, affirmed at the Council of Constantinople in 381.

[20] Arguments by some that the word *form* refers to Christ's "very nature" are unconvincing because they inevitably can't take the phrase "form of a servant" in the same way they want to

take the phrase "form of God." While the Old and New Testaments do not use this language of earthly kings, they did think of the king as God's Son (e.g., 2 Samuel 7:14; Psalm 2:7) and even could refer to him as "God" (e.g., Psalm 45:6). I conclude that the phrase has royal overtones.

[21] So the Jewish writer Philo on the *logos*, *Who is the Heir of Divine Things* 206 (translation taken from the Loeb classical series, F. H. Colson, trans., *Philo IV* (Cambridge: Cambridge University, 1932).

[22] A bracketed comment in the New International Version at the end of Mark after 16:8.

[23] We call this translation the Septuagint.

[24] Before the Council of Chalcedon that set Christianity's view of Christ as fully human and fully divine was another council at Ephesus in 449, the "Robber" Council. We don't hear much of it anymore because it affirmed Eutychianism, which we now view as a heresy. In other words, despite certain politics that tried to establish the decisions of this dead end council, they did not stand the test of time. Eutychianism was not the direction in which God was leading the church.

[25] A favorite line of mine from a hymn, *Spirit of God, Descend Upon my Heart* (George Croly, *Psalms and Hymns for Public Worship* [London: 1854]).

Conclusion
So Who Decides?

We began our pilgrimage with a question: "Who decides what the Bible means?" This question led us to ponder the flexibility of words and the "dictionaries" we bring to the interpretation of the Bible. We talked about our very individual ways of looking at the world and the glasses our church groups wear. We discussed culture and scholars. Lastly we discussed the church.

In the course of our journey we came across three basic reasons for the very diverse interpretations of the Bible we find among Christians today. All these reasons grow from the very nature of words themselves and the Bible's words in particular. We define words not on the basis of some absolute meaning but by the way they are used, their context. This fact creates a situation in which the meaning of a word can change from one instance to the next. The "dictionary" I bring to a word determines the meaning I see in it.

Thus the first reason for the diversity of interpretations comes from the fact that the original meaning of the Bible's words was a function of the dictionaries of its original audiences. In other words, the original meaning of Romans was a function of how the ancient Christian Paul and this ancient audience in Rome used words. Since our cultural dictionary is often vastly different from theirs, we have a situation where we are prone to misunderstand the original meaning without even realizing it.

A second reason is the fact that there are so many different books in the Bible, all of whose individual meanings were a function of their original contexts. There are countless ways to connect the teaching of these individual books to one another. The process of integrating the meanings of these texts is one that takes place completely outside the text. It is something I do as an interpreter from the outside looking in. The Bible itself by and large does not tell me how to connect its teaching together.

Finally, it is not always clear how to connect these ancient meanings to today even if I know them. Again, the books of the Bible do not tell us how to reapply their teaching to today. These books were largely unaware that people like me would later read them in so different a world. They do not stop to tell me how their comments might play out in a different setting. All these factors come together to create the incredible diversity of Christian interpretations.

So what dictionary do I bring to the Bible's words so that they will take on an authoritative meaning? The simple answer is the dictionary of the Holy Spirit—the definitions that God brings to my mind as I read the text. Such events of revelation can certainly take place for individuals. God can make the words of the Bible come alive to me, with the Bible as a kind of sacrament and means of his gracious revelation. But there are dangers here as well. What if I am wrongly convinced of what God is saying?

If each individual has the Spirit, then I am on safer ground when I try to hear God's voice in communion with other Christians. Presumably the more Christians I am in fellowship with, the more Spirit we share between us. I can certainly hear God's voice in a particular church group or denomination. God can bring particular groups to emphasize various dimensions of the overall truth, even truths that might "cancel each other out" if there were only one Christian group. But there are also the dangers of divisiveness, self-sufficiency, and error here as well. What if my group is on the wrong track?

If the Spirit of God inhabits the whole body of Christ, then I am on safest ground when I read the Bible with the saints of all the ages, past and present. This pushes me to read the Bible through the eyes of Christian consensus and tradition, more than with a view to the original meaning. The original meaning was a valid meaning, and it is important for Christians to have some understanding of the original meaning to give us depth.

But if the original meaning is the center of God's voice, then most of the Christians throughout the ages, including most Christians today, are largely deaf to it. The modern tools of biblical studies are valid, and they can lead us to true understandings about the early church and the historical Jesus. But there are also great uncertainties about the original meaning. And even when we are certain, it is not always immediately obvious how those meanings translate to the church of today.

If we are honest with ourselves, we have read the Scripture this way all along. We did it before the modern era without realizing it. Fundamentalists insist they are reading the original meaning and not relying on the church, but they are sneaking in the traditions of orthodoxy in the way they define the words. Evangelicals painstakingly do their homework, try to determine the original meaning, and then subtly sneak in these canons of orthodoxy and faith when they make the leap from that time to our time.

In the end, the appropriation of the Bible in the church amounts to two things. The first is the constraints and boundaries that the consensus of the church has placed upon it as God has spoken and continues to speak through the ages. Regardless of the original meaning of the Bible, we are in trouble if we do not assent to these. The second is the ethic of love that formed the heart of Jesus' ethic in the New Testament. Any interpretation of the Bible that justifies hatred is inappropriate. These are the boundaries that the "dictionary of the Spirit" has set for us. If we read the Bible with these glasses, we will not go wrong!

The Book in a Nutshell

1. More foundational than the question of *whether* the Bible is authoritative is the question of *which interpretation* is authoritative.

2. My faltering human reason is *always* involved when I am interpreting Scripture.

3. The meaning of a word depends on how it is used in a specific context. Words do not correspond neatly to things in the world or to some universal, timeless dictionary.

4. The idea that we might base our beliefs on "Scripture alone" often reflects a misunderstanding of how works work and of how its books came together.

5. The books of the Bible did not *originally* address anyone alive today.

6. We would have to make extensive entries into our "dictionary" to come anywhere close to understanding the precise nuances a book like 1 Corinthians had originally.

7. The Bible ultimately is not the controlling factor in what a Christian believes.

8. Many Christians treat the words of the Bible as somewhat "magical" words designed to take on hidden meanings.

9. At best these are instances of God inspiring the words to become the words of God to an individual. But these meanings are not what the words originally meant.

10. The authority of the Bible's words is only as legitimate as the dictionary you bring to the words.

11. The Bible is a dangerous tool in the hands of some individuals, because it is easy to make the words say what you want them to say.

12. The New Testament frequently reads the words of the Old Testament out of context to one degree or another. It often reads the words in terms of Christ.

13. The way the New Testament itself interprets the Old creates an inner conflict for those who say the literal meaning of the Bible is the only authoritative meaning for

us. When we interpret the Bible literally, we find that the Bible does not interpret itself literally.

14. Some would suggest that God hid countless meanings in the words of Scripture just waiting to jump out at Christians at various times and places.

15. We inherit "guidelines of faith" from the Christian traditions around us, rules for the kinds of meanings we "are allowed" to see in the words of Scripture.

16. The Bible can take on a sacramental quality where it becomes a means of experiencing God's gracious revelation. Ordinary words are transformed into the voice of God.

17. You can almost always find some verse that at least sounds like it supports your church's position.

18. There will always be verses that at least sound like they are in tension with the positions of your group, "naughty" verses. Such verses are deemphasized and redefined so that they do not interfere with the group's overall "paradigm," its way of processing the world.

19. The Bible is more like a library of books than a single book.

20. Reading the Bible as a single book leads us to read it consistently out of context.

21. It is a subtle narcissism to think that the meanings of the individual books of the Bible have to fit easily with one another from my perspective.

22. The final step of integrating the Bible's diverse teaching, the most important step in deciding what the Bible means as a whole, is one that the Bible itself does not tell us how to take.

23. Placed within the context of the "New" Testament, the words of the Jewish Bible become the "Old" Testament and take on new meanings in their new context.

24. Is it possible that God is so big and beyond our understanding that "he" can only be brought within our view by irreconcilable paradoxes and metaphors?

25. Maybe some of the diversity among different denominations is a help to the limitations of our human understanding.

26. We lose something when we force the meanings of individual books together, frequently creating a meaning that *none* of the books had.

27. There is always more than one way to translate words from one language to another.

28. No translation can do complete justice to the original meaning because our culture doesn't come equipped with all the same categories as those of the Bible's original cultures.

29. We bring cultural assumptions to every page of the Bible, often without realizing it.

30. The questions we bring to the Biblical text determine the answers we find there, and these usually have more to do with our context than with those of the original audiences.

31. We fill in the gaps of the story with filler that makes sense given our cultural and theological assumptions. We connect the pieces with the glue of our perspectives on life and the world. The words and stories take on a mirror quality in which, by the Spirit, we see ourselves and our lives.

32. Christian men who don't greet each other in church with a kiss and Christian women who don't veil their heads in prayer implicitly acknowledge that some of the biblical material was written to address a different culture.

33. Doing what the ancients did is not doing what they did if the significance of the action is different.

34. The Bible itself as a whole does not model an unchanging ethic.

35. Except for the command to love, neither Jesus nor Paul were legalistic or absolutist in their appropriation of Scripture.

36. To be faithful to God's Spirit, we must be flexible in the way we appropriate Scripture, allowing both for exceptional circumstances and changing cultures.

37. **Guideline 1: Any appropriation of the Bible that is in keeping with love of our neighbor is appropriate; any appropriation that involves hatred of a person is not Christian.**

38. If we have to know the original meaning to hear God's voice in Scripture, then the vast majority of Christians who have lived for the last two thousand years are in trouble.

39. We simply do not have enough information on the original contexts of these individual writings to conclude definitively on countless different issues.

40. We face the ongoing possibility that some new evidence or hypothesis will completely revolutionize the perspectives about which scholars are currently so convinced.

41. Despite current scholarly confidence on many issues, in the end we can never be certain that we have it right.

42. Hypotheses are pictures we draw out of the dots that are available to us. A good hypothesis sticks closely to the available dots and forms the heart of its picture from them.

43. The next generation of scholars may look back at the current scholarly paradigms in puzzlement.

44. Christian tradition has always played a role in the legitimate appropriation of Scripture.

45. Human reasoning and experience are always factors in our appropriation of the Bible. They are the "round house" through which all the trains of knowledge pass.

46. If God's Spirit lives in the body of Christ, then it is when we are in fellowship with the church of the ages that we are most likely to hear God's Spirit on any particular belief or practice.

47. We would not have a New Testament if there had not been a church to collect and recognize the authority of its books.

48. Those who believe that the books in our Bibles are authoritative must at least believe that God worked in the church beyond the New Testament in this one area.

49. The Bible itself models the idea that God sometimes unfolds his revelation over long periods of time and even tailors it for particular phases of history.

50. God sometimes gave instruction in the Bible that accommodated particular audiences—even though it wasn't his ideal.

51. God brought the church to affirm a number of things about Christ *after* the New Testament.

52. The New Testament alone could not settle the great Trinitarian and Christological debates of the 300's and 400's. Its original meaning was insufficient to arbitrate between the major options of these debates.

53. Ironically, the desire to make the original meaning of the Bible the ultimate source of what we believe repeatedly leads some scholars to play games with the original meaning. Such scholars force their interpretations to agree with legitimate beliefs that really come from God's inspiration of the church beyond the pages of the Bible.

54. God's movement in the church is patient. Sometimes he accommodates the hard-heartedness of generations. Sometimes he meets cultures with context-specific beliefs and practices.

55. We recognize God's movement best when we look back at the Spirit's working in the church over time.

56. **Guideline 2: Any interpretation that fits with the faith of the church throughout the ages is an appropriate interpretation whether it is the original meaning or not.**